THE FARMER'S WIFE

THE FARMER'S WIFE

The Life and Work of Women on the Land

SIMON BUTLER

HALSGROVE

First published in Great Britain in 2013
Copyright © Simon Butler 2013

British Library Cataloguing-in-Publication Data
A CIP record for this title is available from the British Library

ISBN 978 0 85704 219 4

HALSGROVE
Halsgrove House,
Ryelands Business Park,
Bagley Road, Wellington, Somerset TA21 9PZ
Tel: 01823 653777   Fax: 01823 216796
email: sales@halsgrove.com

Part of the Halsgrove group of companies
Information on all Halsgrove titles is available at: www.halsgrove.com

Printed and bound in China by Everbest Printing Co Ltd

Contents

DEDICATION

For Ann Myrtle Painter

Foreword

Three summer's since I chose a maid,
Too young may be - but more's to do
At harvest time than bide and woo.

'The Farmer's Bride'
Charlotte Mary Mew

This is a curious book to embark upon for of course there is no single story to tell for each farming wife will have a different tale; and this is as true of women in farming today as it has been down through the centuries. What if anything binds them collectively is the work that women on the land traditionally undertook and it is this theme that is followed here. And while the detail of their work has inevitably changed over the centuries, there persists, even up to present times, faint echoes of long-established practices.

While the main title suggests I write only about the woman married to the farmer, the book's subtitle makes clear that it also includes women's work on the land, and indeed at times the theme widens to look at the life of women in rural Britain more generally. It also touches on the lives of country children for not only did the nurturing of boys and girls fall principally on their mothers, work considered fit for women was also work considered fit for their children too. I have attempted to provide a countrywide flavour but if the book errs on the side of the Westcountry I can only offer the excuse that this is where I grew up and now live.

The scope of this book however is not to look too much into the distant past but rather to look at that period in history when the 'mysterious lady' is revealed in actuality through the medium of photography; a period when revolutions in science coincided with the social revolutions in western culture, culminating in a world war that, ironically, turned out to be a war of liberation for women in both labour and suffrage.

It was after the First World War that mechanisation began to change forever the face of farming, and changed too the men and women of the land.

Acknowledgements

Thanks are due to those who have inspired and encouraged me in the writing of this book, foremost my family and friends, to Mairi, Tom and Christian Hunt for photographs from their family albums, and to everyone at Halsgrove who have supported this project from the outset.

The book would not have been possible without access to the thousands of photographs made available through the Halsgrove Community History Series, many of which appear in this book. My thanks go to the authors and contributors to this series, literally too many to mention by name, but I recommend readers to seek out the individual books. There are now over 220 titles in the series details of which can be found at www.halsgrove.com. Other photographs are taken from the author's personal collection.

Particular thanks are due to Luke Smith for his photograph of the kitchen at Roseweek Farm, to Peter Brears who was generous in allowing me use of his cutaway drawings from his book *The Old Devon Farmhouse*. Thanks also to Delores Morrow of the Montana Historical Society for help in obtaining the photographs of Evelyn Cameron.

Books and articles referred to in preparing this title are included in the bibliography.

Introduction

I remember, I remember
The house where I was born,
The little window where the sun
Came peeping in at morn.
                          Thomas Hood

This book does no more than give an impressionistic picture of the world of women who farmed and worked on the land. Of the millions who laboured, each has an individual and different story, the commonality being the daily tasks they performed. In early times, poverty and sickness would be a common factor in their lives, long days of dull labour in a world confined by how far one might walk in a day, forever at the mercy of the weather, where a poor summer might determine life or death. Yet it is from this harsh existence that springs the defining characteristic of country-women through the centuries – resourcefulness. Those who listened most carefully

The kitchen at Roseweek Farm in Cornwall in the 1980s with Molly Trist and her son Terry who took over the farm when his father, Charlie, died.

at their parents' knee absorbed the priceless knowledge that, in their turn, gave them self-reliance. That a woman's family prospered, indeed survived, rested on a compendium of learning as deep-rooted as any desert-dweller's.

It survives today in some – in those who through generations of farming have forged an unbroken line of wisdom. For others it plays no part in their lives; and in any case today's farming wife needs to know different things, also vital.

I was fortunate to witness the last of the 'old days' of farming, helping out where I could as a boy on a small farm run by Charlie and Molly Trist and their son Terry in Cornwall in the 1960s. Milking was still done by hand, hen's eggs collected from hedgerow nests, small fields of potatoes and barley planted, and threshing done on an antique machine that had seen more engines powered by steam than with diesel.

An ancient Fordson thumped its way around the fields where horse-drawn binders and seed drills lay not-long abandoned, now rusting under the Cornish sun. The farmhouse had few mod cons, a Rayburn cooker and inside lavatory, but water dribbled in from a collecting tank away in the top field, often running dangerously low in the summertime. A small town was a few minutes away with every kind of goods available, but the farm itself could have survived within its own small world had the need arisen.

Because the position of women in society placed them as second-class citizens throughout history it shouldn't be assumed that our notional farmer's wife felt anything but in control of her circumstances, proud of the part she played in the farming household. Charged with the injunction that she was playing a subservient, even demeaning role, I can picture what Molly Trist would have done: dust the flour off her hands on her pinny and shoo me unceremoniously out of her kitchen.

These memories provide the background to this book.

Simon Butler
Manaton 2013

The Mysterious Lady

And Ruth the Moabite said to Naomi: "Let me now go to the field,
and glean ears of corn after him in whose sight I shall find favor."
And she said to her: "Go, my daughter."

The Book of Ruth 2:2

History is the domain of men. Brute strength, culture, religion and the law have determined it so for centuries. Certainly in the earliest written records it is rare to find specific references to women in farming, and while the place of the farmer in the literature is assured, the farmer's wife, his daughters and women working on the land in general is a story largely untold. Historians are playing their part in rectifying this and we are beginning to unravel the question why the role of the woman has often remained, until recent times, hidden.

The Gleaners by Jean-Francois Millet, 1857. The theme is an eternal one, linked to the story of Ruth in the Old Testament.

'Ruth in Boaz' Field' (detail) by Julius Schnorr Von Carolsfield, 1828.

It is interesting to note that when Millet's painting 'The Gleaners' was first exhibited at the Paris Salon in 1857, it was met with disapproval and suspicion by the critics. Though the theme was well-understood, echoing the biblical tale of Ruth and the centuries-old right of poor women and children to forage for grain left in the fields following the harvest, the upper classes in France viewed it with disgust. It was a unwelcome reminder that French society was built upon the labour of the working masses – and in this case women! As one critic put it 'Millet's three gleaners have gigantic pretensions, they pose as the Three Fates of Poverty… their ugliness and their grossness unrelieved.'

As for the Bible itself, the place of the woman was clear. They were the property of fathers and husbands and their daily duties pre-ordained. This is not to suggest their work was any more onerous than that of the men, or that most men had any more sense of freedom than women. Rights and privileges trickled down from the ruling classes and the majority of labouring men were themselves often little more than slaves.

What preceded biblical times we rely upon archaeology to relate. The accepted view of prehistoric societies is that of the hunter-gatherer, when the men went out to hunt while the women stayed behind looking after hearth and home, tending to domestic duties such as those that had to be fulfilled on a daily basis: spinning, food preparation and preservation, making garments from fibres and skins.

Among their most important tasks was the collection of water, a role of women in many primitive societies even today, and certainly by some in Britain well into the twentieth century. It is probable that in the transition from nomadic life towards a more stable pastoral culture, women retained those activities that were more sedentary and perhaps required less muscular strength. Pottery, spindle whorls, pot-boiling stones and similar artefacts provide clues as to the everyday domestic life of our prehistoric ancestors.

As these primitive societies learned to grow crops and domesticate animals, the need to constantly move in search of food diminished. Instead, people began to live in settled communities, tending fields or raising animals on nearby land. They built stronger, more permanent homes, surrounding their settlements with walls to protect themselves.

Whether nomadic or sedentary, and irrespective of muscle power, cultural mores or tribal law, it remained the fact that as it was the woman who gestated, gave birth, and fed her child that this cemented the woman's place alongside hearth and home. Little wonder then that work traditionally ascribed to the woman should reside in that place too.

*　*　*

The Romans brought their own brand of slavery to Britain, a country in which slavery was already common among the tribes. The Roman attitude to women was generally that they and their children were second class citizens for whom few rights were reserved. In Roman law there were more restrictions on women than on men and women were effectively the property of fathers and husbands. Britons as Roman subjects could look for little in the way of rights, other than that if they followed the law they would be protected.

We get some fascinating glimpses of day-to-day life on a Roman farm from the writings of various historians of the day, although yet again women are conspicuous by their absence in such records. The historian Marcus Terentius Varro (116–27BC) drew on his practical experience in agriculture to create *Res Rusticae*; three books each treating one of the three principles: agriculture, viticulture and livestock.

Res Rusticae is a lively first-hand account of Roman farms and farming from the first century BC, with advice on how to treat slaves, run a wealthy villa, grow crops and tend cattle. While throughout the author refers almost exclusively to male workers and their duties on the farm through the seasons, the elderly Varro addresses the work to Fundania, his wife, who will be left with the running of a farm as soon he 'must pack his baggage for departure from this life'.

There is however a direct reference to the 'housekeeper' from which it is possible to surmise that such a role was exclusively a female one:

References to farming in writings and images from Roman times are dominated by men; here a mosaic of an ox cart and its male driver.

The 'Tellus' panel from the Ara Pacis Augustae, *the 'Altar of Augustan Peace' in Rome. The central figure is usually identified as Mother Earth, or as Ceres, the Roman goddess of grain and the harvest, and associated motherly relationships*

13

'Ceres Teaching Agriculture to King Triptolemus,' a painting by Jean Francois Lagrenée (1724–1805). Ceres (Demeter in Greek myths) is said to have instructed Triptolemus in the art of agriculture, while he is credited with the invention of the plough.

The Duties of the Housekeeper
The overseer should be responsible for the duties of the housekeeper. If the master has given her to you for a wife, you should be satisfied with her, and she should respect you. Require that she be not given to wasteful habits; that she does not gossip with the neighbours and other women. She should not receive visitors either in the kitchen or in her own quarters. She should not go out to parties, nor should she gad about. She should not practise religious observances, nor should she ask others to do so for her without the permission of the master or the mistress. Remember that the master practises religion for the entire household. She should be neat in appearance and should keep the house swept and garnished. Every night before she goes to bed she should see that the hearth is swept and clean. On the Kalends, the Ides, the Nones, and on all feast days, she should hang a garland over the hearth. On those days also she should pray fervently to the household gods. She should take care that she has food cooked for you and for the hands. She should have plenty of chickens and an abundance of eggs. She should diligently put up all kinds of preserves every year.

Note that it is a male overseer who controls the farm and that it was not at all unusual for the 'master' (the landowner) to have 'given' the housekeeper to the overseer as a wife – a neat arrangement which would help ensure the pair's mutual responsibility in carrying out their respective duties. It also emphasises the place of the woman in Roman society as little more than a chattel; part and parcel of the master's property.

And as we shall find, whether 'wife' or 'housekeeper', in later centuries the domestic duties of a first-century Roman woman hardly differed from that of the farmer's wife 1500 years later. Preparation of food, cooking, and ensuring an adequate supply for the future remain the major domestic preoccupations of the farming wife through the centuries, and it was not until the development of an industrialised food supply, canned food and the invention of the refrigerator, that this changed.

For the Roman housekeeper the raw materials of fresh meat, fish and vegetables came from their immediate surroundings, but she would also be adept in the preservation of foodstuffs to be kept through the winter months when fresh produce was in short supply. Smoking, drying and salting were the principal means, with salt being a precious commodity, often paid as part of a man's wages and from which we get our word 'salary'. Rock salt (*sal facitum*) and sea salt (*sal navitum*) were used for dry-salting and pickling, particular for meat such as ham and for fish. Eggs were also preserved by covering them with fine salt.

Meat and fish would also be smoked, thus prolonging their edible life. Fruit was preserved by drying it in the sun, as were some vegetables, and the pickling of food in wine or vinegar was also practiced. A type of fish sauce was popular, known to the Romans as *garum*. This involved placing the gills, intestines and blood of the fish in an open jar and saturating it with salt. Vinegar, parsley, wine and sweet herbs were added and this mixture then exposed to the hot sun until the fish parts rotted down into a liquid. After two or three months the sauce was ready to be bottled and used.

*　　*　　*

The Roman preoccupation with infrastructure saw roads, civic and domestic buildings, and aqueducts transforming the British landscape during their 400 years of occupation. For those working on the land the Romans brought in new farming methods, standardising crop production and introducing more sophisticated equipment. The British climate was less than ideal for Mediterranean farming and in the century following the Claudian invasion the Roman historian Tacitus paints an all too familiar picture of our weather:

A Roman bronze figurine depicting a man ploughing with oxen. Almost certainly the Romans introduced a more sophisticated plough and yokes for oxen into Britain.

> *Their sky is obscured by continual rain and cloud. Severity of cold is unknown. The days exceed in length those of our part of the world; the nights are bright, and in the extreme north so short that between sunlight and dawn you can perceive but a slight distinction...*
>
> *With the exception of the olive and vine, and plants which usually grow in warmer climates, the soil will yield, and even abundantly, all ordinary produce. It ripens indeed slowly, but is of rapid growth, the cause in each case being the same, namely, the excessive moisture of the soil and of the atmosphere.*

The depth of the Roman influence was such that it survives to this day, not least in many place names, in parts of our language and our administrative systems. The majority of those invaders who followed them, including Saxons, Danes and Normans, followed the Romans' lead in their plans to establish Britain as part of their wider Empire, while the subsequent ruling elites, kings, queens, lord protectors and archbishops among them – all drew on the example set by those first imperial overlords.

The Dark Ages, so-called for their lack of written records rather than the actuality of a period of unrelieved gloom, provide little evidence of change in farming practices for, come the dawn of the period we call the Middle Ages, we find farming being carried on much as before. Only with the arrival of the Normans are we given a clearer picture of life on the land although specific references to the role played by women are sparse. In two of the greatest surviving documents from this time women are conspicuous by their absence.

William the Conqueror's defeat of King Harold at Hastings in 1066 was later celebrated in the construction of the Bayeux Tapestry, a remarkable depiction of the events leading up to the conquest. Said to have been commissioned by William's wife, Queen Matilda, there remains some doubt as to who made it and where, but

'Here King Harold has been killed' reads the embroidered text on this panel of the Bayeux Tapestry.

One of only three women depicted in the Bayeux Tapestry is seen here escaping (with a child?) from a house that is being torched by William's soldiers. Other women appearing elsewhere are Edith, wife of Edward the Confessor and sister of King Harold, and Aelfgyva, a figure otherwise referred to as 'The Mysterious Lady'.

few other records are so immediately graphic in their illustration of life in the late eleventh century. Measuring 70 metres in length it contains 626 human figures, 190 horses, 35 dogs and 506 birds and other animals. And 3 women.

Without drawing too many conclusions from this absence, after all much of the story told revolves around military conquest, it is some measure of the male dominance of society at that time and one can assume that even if the female figured little in the upper echelon of the social scale, then she certainly played a vital role down in the village.

The suppression of the female presence by officialdom is further supported by examination of the second great document from this period, the Domesday Book in which only a handful of women's names are recorded. After the Conquest the Norman predisposition for male-domination meant women could no longer hold land and many Anglo-Saxon noblewomen were forced from their estates. While single women could through inheritance own property, in law this came to belong to their husbands at the time of their marriage. Many widows and daughters fled to nunneries in order to avoid being forced into marriage with William's soldiers.

Compiled by William in 1086 the Domesday Book was essentially an instrument to record property ownership and through this to impose taxes and for this reason, with a few exceptions, woman are discounted in the records. Of those mentioned the most prominent was Judith, countess of Northumbria and Huntingdon, who was King William's niece. One named Aelgar was granted enough land to live on by the Sheriff of Trent in return for teaching his daughter embroidery. Others are anonymous, such as the one 'poor woman' of Barfreston in Kent who only appears because she had to make an annual payment of 3¾d, although for what is not recorded. Once more we are left with a picture of women being held in thrall to men, fulfilling traditional roles within the household and on the land, duties little changed for centuries and with little prospect of change. Indeed, the everyday and seasonal tasks of women on the land at the time of Domesday changed little for the next 700 years – and have echoes even unto modern times.

Through much of the Middle Ages religion and the law combined to maintain a firm hand controlling the place of women in society, and while some women rose to become noted in history the vast majority are just as invisible to us as the Bayeux Tapestry's own Mystery Woman.

Among those whose stories we know are the women related to royalty, queens and princesses and others of noble birth. Others' names we know through their religious activities, various abbesses who controlled vast estates attached to a convent or nunnery forming independent, self-supporting religious communities. As one observer comments: The abbess 'had to have the administrative skills of a baron and the spiritual authority of a parson.' Medieval nuns had no reason to go beyond the limits of the convent or nunnery for anything, and the growing of food and care of animals mirrored that which went on outside the convent walls. Convents gradually increased in wealth and size coming to form enormous establishments, some having the appearance of a fortified town.

Religious houses provided one arena in which women could excel in Medieval times. This illumination comes from Chaucer's The Canterbury Tales *witten at the end of the fourteenth century. It depicts the Prioress, a position ranking next below the abbess of an abbey.*

In medieval Britain peasant wives and daughters were effectively property of their husbands and fathers but in reality the poorest men and women shared equality through poverty. The feudal system could at least be said to suppress the peasantry equally whatever their sex, and there existed a hierarchy roughly dividing the peasant class into the free and the unfree.

Unfree peasants were not slaves, but as villeins or serfs they had to remain on the manor where they were born, performing compulsory labour in exchange for a modest roof over their head and a small parcel of land. They needed their lord's permission to marry or to move away. They had no legal rights under Common Law and any disputes were to be settled by the lord of the manor.

Unfree peasants were tied to work on the land belonging to their lord. Here two villeins are depicted ploughing with a team of four yoked oxen. From the Luttrell Psalter an illuminated manuscript dated c.1330, held in the British Library.

In return for land they could use to grow their own food villeins were required to work a fixed number of days for their master. Here the Lord of the Manor oversees his workers cutting grain with sickles.

Free peasants did have access to the law. They were able to move, buy and sell land, and manage their own affairs, but their economic conditions were not necessarily much better than those of the villeins.

During the later Middle Ages the distinction between free and unfree peasantry became blurred, villeins could for a payment buy themselves out of the strictures imposed by the Lord of the Manor and intermarriage between the free and unfree became more common. Couples most often married in their early twenties, or even (following the Black Death) in their late teens.

In the home

Here the first duty of the villein's housewife would be to ensure that food and drink was available for her family. Hunger was ever present and available foodstuffs were dependent upon the season, with a soup-like frumenty providing a universal dish that could be prepared and left to cook over the open fire while other tasks were completed. Made primarily from boiling cracked wheat various vegetable ingredients could be added to provide flavour. When meat was available the whole could be made into a pottage – sometimes serving as the main meal over a period of days. Bread was a staple but expensive, especially as the ownership of a quern – a hand tool for milling grain – was outlawed in the medieval period with all grain having to be taken to a licenced mill for which a payment was required and tax collected. Consequently the miller was universally disliked, a medieval joke running:

Q. What is the boldest thing in the world?
A. A miller's shirt, for every day it clasps a thief by the throat.

Iron or bronze cauldrons such as this were the principal means of cooking over open fires and their design remained largely unchanged for centuries.

Making ale was another of the housewife's daily tasks. Water was often of dubious quality and drinking it provided no sustenance. Malted barley stirred slowly in water in a large bowl over an open fire gradually released its sugar; when strained off and with yeast added the mixture was left to ferment for a day or so before being ready to drink.

Domestic arrangements were spartan. A single dwelling space with rough-hewn benches and tables, if any, and cots for sleeping. Central to the home was a fireplace, an open hearth in which the embers of a fire would be continually kept from dying, being brought back to life whenever a pot was to be boiled. Various irons, hung above or next to the fire to provide support for cooking pots, and a brand-iron on which to stand the hot cauldron. Many of these utensils survived well into the nineteenth century, hardly changed from medieval times.

Turf and faggots were the principal fuels (villeins usually had rights of turbary and permission to collect fallen wood for their fires, along with other benefits strictly controlled by their manorial lord). An iron cauldron provided the main source for cooking, with a brick or clay oven, fired by dried gorse or similar material, for baking. Food was served in simple earthenware bowls and eaten with wooden spoons.

During the day sunlight shone through unglazed, shuttered windows and doorways; at night rush lights provided dim illumination.

If the housewife was caring for a baby nursing would be done while other duties were performed: clothes to be mended, spinning and weaving, the care and feeding of animals (usually chickens, a sow and sometimes a cow), and the tending of a small garden plot that yielded a variety of vegetables, 'edible weeds' including vetch, and herbs such as hyssop. These plots and a store-pit of grain were often all that stood between the household and starvation.

The late medieval poem *Piers Plowman* by William Langland (c.1332–c.1386), vividly describes the grim life of the medieval peasant woman:

A peasant woman feeding chicks and mother hen (note the cord around its leg suggesting just how valuable these animals were to the household). At the same time as emptying grain from a bowl the woman holds a distaff tucked under her arm from which hangs a drop spindle. This simple arrangement allowed the housewife to continue spinning yarn while carrying out other household duties.

Burdened with children and landlords' rent;
What they can put aside from what they make spinning they spend on housing,
Also on milk and meal to make porridge with
To sate their children who cry out for food
And they themselves also suffer much hunger,
And woe in wintertime, and waking up nights
To rise on the bedside to rock the cradle,
Also to card and comb wool, to patch and to wash,
To rub flax and reel yarn and to peel rushes
That it is pity to describe or show in rhyme
The woe of these women who live in huts.

In the fields

The traditional round of the farming year, preparing the soil, sowing, weeding, reaping and winnowing called on all hands including women and children. The heaviest work would naturally fall upon the strongest men and boys, and over time specific tasks appear to fall into the domain either of men or of women.

Agrarian literature is full of references to the plough*man*, the woods*man* and so on, activities that predominantly are seen as masculine, while the very term 'husbandry' speaks for itself. The reality is that women too adopted specific roles on the land, firstly those in which their proximity to the home and hearth allowed both domestic and farming tasks to be done together and those to which the female temperament might be said to be more conducive, the care and nurturing of young animals for instance. Such gender-specific tasks became so ingrained in the culture of farming that they have persisted even to the present day.

The yearly round in medieval farming; an early illumination depicting ploughing in March.

The top panel of this medieval illumination showing a man broadcasting seed and a women spinning yarn, the bottom panel a man harrowing soil in preparation for sowing seed. Well before this time the roles of men and women in agriculture had already begun to be defined.

For the medieval farming wife these tasks including milking sheep, goats and perhaps a cow if one was owned by the family from which butter would be made. Cheese was usually made from sheep or goats' milk and could be found in various forms: hard and soft, green cheese (soft cheese made from compressed curds) and a variety known as 'spermyse' in which curds were flavoured with herbs and their juices.

Daily work with sheep and goats would include the care of the animals when they gave birth and the nurturing of sickly or orphaned lambs for instance. Carding and spinning of wool was also a role taken by the woman, although shearing was traditionally undertaken by the men. Children were often employed as shepherds if stock was taken out on to the heath or common for grazing and were used as bird scarers to protect newly sown crops.

Harvesting was done by all as timing was crucial. Sudden rainstorms and gales could ruin a crop and so cutting, drying and safe transport away from the fields was critical. Gleaning, as we have seen, was a task left to women and children who also took a hand in winnowing, that is the separation of the grain itself from the chaff.

Women too were expected to have a keen knowledge of wild plants, both those used for food and those for medicinal purposes. The countryside was literally a larder for those to whom hunger was never far away and the gathering of plants, fruits and herbs in season, and their preservation through drying and other techniques, stood the family in good stead during long winter months.

In the village

Towards the end of the fourteenth century the pattern of English villages and towns had begun to take on a shape that remained recognisable for centuries to come.

Women milking sheep in a pen. The women on the right are carrying milk and cheese.

Indeed it was not until the development of the railways, and later road transport, that settlements in rural Britain began to take on an aspect much different from their medieval origins. Here we distinguish the 'town' from the manorial desmense, the latter being the agricultural lands worked by peasants, their dwellings and associated mills, bakeries, farm buildings and the manor house itself.

Often centred on a geographical feature such as a river crossing, or a hilltop that afforded defence, towns grew around convenient meeting places for people in the surrounding area, as centres for religious worship and civic control, and as market-places. Merchants arrived with goods for sale, tradesmen set up their weekly market stalls and local craftsmen erected permanent dwellings from which they sold their wares.

Though the land often remained in the hands of the local lord, freemen were able to rent, build or purchase property, and while married women were not legally entitled to own landed property (it passed into the hands of the husband upon marriage), single and widowed women were able to buy and sell land, participate in the world of business, and take over a trade should their husband die.

As with farming, crafts that required muscle power resided largely in the hands of men, although widows are known to have taken over from their blacksmith husbands. The growth of the medieval craft guilds resulted in many crafts permanently resting with men and thus the trades of bakers, millers, weavers, butchers, fishmongers, cordwainers, tailors and vintners are male dominated. It is certain however that women participated in all of these businesses if only behind the scenes. In other spheres, such as brewing for instance, the alewife is thought to have outnumbered men as owners of their business and evidence suggests that women brewed as much if not more ale and beer served in the Middle Ages than men.

Women carding, combing and weaving wool.

A cloth merchant bargains over sacks of woollen fleeces with a member of the Merchant Wool Guild. Medieval craft and merchant guilds were largely the province of men although a widely accepted law known as femme sole *allowed women to trade in their own right, a right not commonly exercised except in the case of a widow continuing her husband's craft.*

Life and death

Death was ever present. Primitive methods of food storage, rotting meat and fish made families already malnourished, subject to disease. Child mortality rates in this period are said to be 30 per cent, some say as high as 50 per cent. It was therefore important to have children so that some might survive into adulthood, although in times of famine women could be simply too small and undernourished to conceive.

Sex was considered a natural part of life, though lust was sinful, and religion played a role in maintaining the notion that sexual pleasure in itself was sinful. Sexual intercourse outside marriage, though common, was prohibited by the teaching of the church and adultery was punishable by law. Physiologically little was understood about the woman's body and popular notions of how babies were conceived led to a variety of bizarre beliefs and practices. Midwifery was practiced informally, the role filled by a woman experienced and trusted within the community, although the success rate was not high and many women died during childbirth. In the thirteenth and fourteenth centuries life expectancy for a woman was as low as 25 years and, as a consequence, led to a preponderance of 4 males to every 3 females.

Likewise medicine was based as much upon magic and religion as on science, though folk medicine and the use of various herbs is known to have been effective in many instances for mild ailments, cuts and bruises. Diseases such as leprosy, typhoid and cholera could decimate small communities when it struck and, with no conception of how such diseases were carried, remedies often relied on black magic and prayer.

In the years following the Conqueror's invasion the population grew from an estimated 1 million to between 5 and 7 million in 1300 – a staggering increase but one that underlines the wealth and productivity of the country under harsh but stable Norman rule. Towns and villages grew, commerce flourished.

Then in 1315 came a prolonged period of catastrophic climate change, starting in that year with a cold and wet spring and a summer when crops failed. The harvest remained poor for another two years causing the Great Famine of 1315–17. In fact for almost a decade the whole of Europe was in the grip of the famine in which millions died, bringing to an end the period of growth and prosperity.

Hardly had the country recovered than a further catastrophe was visited upon the people of Britain, and one that no amount of imprecation to the Almighty could ward off. The Black Death, a plague so virulent that, according to recent research, it wiped out almost half the population of Britain, arrived on these shores in June 1348. It swept through the country at a rate of over one kilometre a day and in a little over a year it had reached the farthest corners of the land. It was a turning point in the history of the kingdom and of life on the land; also a time in which the freedom of individuals began to emerge from beneath the yoke of feudalism.

Life was often brutal and short for the peasantry and sickness and disease ever present. A medieval illumination 'Death and the Shepherdess' depicts a partially-shrouded skeleton brandishing a scythe. The shepherdess hardly has time to say farewell to her little dog before Death grabs her hand to carry her away. Death sings:

'I will not leave you behind.
Come along, take my hand,
Listen, pretty Shepherdess,
We walk along hand in hand.
You won't go to the fields any more,
    morning or evening,
To watch the sheep and care for your
    animals.
There will be nothing left of you
    tomorrow.
After the vigils come the holidays.'

The Turn of the Year

After night's thunder far away had rolled
The fiery day had a kernel sweet of cold,
And in the perfect blue the clouds uncurled,
Like the first gods before they made the world.
'Haymaking' Edward Thomas

While royal dynasties rose and fell in the four centuries between what we know as the end of the late Middle Ages and the main period covered in this book, day-to-day life and work on farms continued much as before. Of course the farming landscape changed, medieval strip farming of the open-field system giving way to small farmsteads under individual ownership and large estates governed by wealthy landowners. Sizeable areas of the country were designated as commonland on which ground the inhabitants held traditional rights of grazing, collecting firewood and cutting turf. Now successive Acts of Parliament saw much of this land 'enclosed', that is brought in to private ownership, often accompanied by resistance, riots and blood-

The medieval villein and his wife would have recognised almost all the elements of this Yorkshire farmyard in 1900 despite the passage of four centuries. Horse power has taken over from oxen but perhaps their biggest surprise would be expressed at the size of the animals – considerably larger than the stock bred by the farmer in the Middle Ages. This was due to the work of the eighteenth century agricultural pioneers who established a scientific approach to stock improvement through selective breeding.

23

shed. The Enclosure Acts have indeed generally been painted as the rich landowners swindling the poor and even as late as the 1940s George Orwell writes condemning this 'lawful theft':

> *Stop to consider how the so-called owners of the land got hold of it. They simply seized it by force, afterwards hiring lawyers to provide them with title-deeds. In the case of the enclosure of the common lands, which was going on from about 1600 to 1850, the land-grabbers did not even have the excuse of being foreign conquerors; they were quite frankly taking the heritage of their own countrymen, upon no sort of pretext except that they had the power to do so.*

As farmers' prosperity grew at the end of the eighteenth century and on into Queen Victoria's reign so the size of their farmhouses grew. In many cases new dwellings were built alongside or in place of the original buildings which then became accommodation for the labourers. Here Clitsome Farm near Roadwater in Somerset is seen around 1880. The family can be seen standing outside the main farmhouse with a thatched workers' cottage and outbuildings on the right.

But the fact was that new agricultural methods demanded a move away from the old farming systems in which intensive land use and repeated annual production of a single crop led to soil exhaustion. This and the rise of the Yeoman Farmer – a distinct breed of men descended from the medieval freeborn commoners whose position in British agriculture grew in strength from the Elizabethan period and who became the backbone of the small landowning class, employing servants and farm labourers of

their own. These farmers, their wives and families, though proud of their working roots rubbed shoulders with the ruling elite, provided younger sons who populated the armed services and the clergy, and daughters who married into the middle classes. Called upon to protect their king and country they were the core participants of well trained bodies of fighting men whose units were among the first to fight on the Western Front, proud descendents of the bowmen of Agincourt.

Lower in social status, there emerged a class of tenant farmers and smallholders, those who worked the land for little more than a subsistence living but whose farmhouse and outbuildings sat adjacent to the land they worked thus forming a coherent agricultural unit. In good times they grew more than was required for their own use, selling the surplus. In bad times they produced enough for themselves supplementing their income by hiring out their labour, or taking in work at home. These are the families who figure most prominently in the following pages.

*   *   *

While there is no such thing as an average farm, regional variations and the size and layout of farm holdings fluctuating widely, we can trace general historic trends in the

Echoes of the past; women haymakers in 1914 at work on the medieval strip fields known as 'lawnsheds' on Portland. Note their traditional dress of white pinafores and bonnets, costume that had changed little for centuries.

The rustic simplicity of Piles Peek farmhouse at Ugborough, Devon c.1890, contrasts with the imposing size of Clitsome house opposite.

Farmers' wives bringing their produce to market on horseback as shown in Thomas Rowlandson's watercolour of Honiton in Devon, dated c.1800. In these days the horse was king, and the pace of the horse governed the pace of life itself.

economic value of farming in the UK, the effects of growth in population, the impact of wars, and the development of new methods and technology. But in all this, the round of daily work on the farm remained constant and tied to the seasons throughout the period from the fifteenth to the nineteenth centuries in which the so-called Agricultural Revolution occurred. Indeed, only the long lens of history provides the perspective to recognise the gradual changes that took place – more evolution than revolution some might say.

Familiar names, Arthur Young, Jethro Tull, Charles 'Turnip' Townshend emerged as leaders in the introduction of new methods such as crop rotation and improved machinery – the invention of the seed drill being the first significant change in agriculture since the abandonment of oxen in favour of the horse.

It was only on the introduction of steam engines that the Agricultural Revolution really got under way and eventually led to industrialised farming as we know it today. These monsters rapidly undermined the hitherto labour-intensive nature of farming, leading to an increase in the size of farms and throwing thousands of men out of work. In a few short decades from the end of the nineteenth century, first steam and then the internal combustion engine, saw the final days of horse power on the farm slip away forever.

Perhaps because artists and writers of the nineteenth century recognised the changing nature of rural Britain they began to romanticise the 'rural idyll' in novels and in paintings as though to capture a lost world. Indeed it is unlikely that such a world ever existed. Painters and novelists mostly chose to ignore the grime and harshness of labour on the farm, and women and young girls in particular were portrayed as having a natural beauty and an innocence untouched by the impurities of urban life. Thomas Hardy describes his heroine in *Tess of the d'Urbervilles*:

A young member of the band turned her head at the exclamation. She was a fine and handsome girl – not handsomer than some others, possibly – but her mobile peony mouth and large innocent eyes added eloquence to colour and shape. She wore a red ribbon in her hair, and was the only one of the white company who could boast of such a pronounced adornment.

Likewise, European artists of the day revelled in the faux pastoralism favoured by the Victorian public and while some did attempt to portray the realities of working life on the land, most were producing highly-romanticised images of women farmers, milkmaids and shepherdesses. This was a far cry from earlier centuries when the 'innocent' country lass was the focus of many of Britain's bawdiest folk songs and a metaphor for the alluring fecundity of the natural world.

'The Young Shepherdess' by Jean-Francois Millet painted in 1873. Such paintings cemented the artist's reputation as an idealistic sentimentalist, though much of his work represented the grimmer side of agricultural life. Here the shepherdess is cleaning a hank of wool with a teasel head, her flock on the hilside beyond.

Throughout the nineteenth century the insipid sentimentalisation of country life often lay in direct contrast to the poverty faced by many. 'The Milkmaid' by Myles Birket Foster, completed in 1899, portrays a handsome young woman with a milk pail on her head returning from the fields.

And Peggy took her milk pails still,
And sang her evening song,
To milk her cows on Cowslip Hill
For half the summer long.
        From 'Peggy's the Lady of the Hall'
        by John Clare.

Once it began, the march of the machines was relentless, populating the landscape like so many alien beasts, devouring forests for their fuel and hedgerows with their appetite for more open land; blackening the air with smoke and noise.

While the Greek inventor Hero had first demonstrated the potential of steam power in the first century AD it was not until the late eighteenth century that truly practical machines began to appear, first in mining where steam pumps were used to clear water from deep mines and, in 1801, Richard Trevithick demonstrated that steam could move a vehicle along a road. By 1825 the first steam railway was opened the advent of which would further change the nature of farming, opening the way to the rapid transport of farm produce to Britain's growing cities.

On farms small stationary engines were used to turn chaff cutters, grist mills and the like and by the mid 1850s steam engines were used for ploughing and threshing. While the operation and maintenance of these machines fell to the men, their increasing appearance in the countryside changed the nature of seasonal tasks such as harvesting which through earlier centuries, while undoubtedly arduous, took place amid the quiet rhythm of scythes and the slow creaking of cartwheels. A successful harvest was reliant upon the strength of many hands, men, women and children, and governed by the clemency of the weather.

A steam engine powers a threshing drum into which sheaves of corn are being fed at a farm near Padstow in Cornwall c.1900. This was exclusively the work of male labourers, often working in gangs and taking their machinery from farm to farm. Yet the traditions of the harvest are continued, the women bringing food and drink out to the fields, here joined by the children no doubt encouraged by the novelty of having their photograph taken.

The whole tackle consisted of the steam engine, the drum in to which the sheaves of corn were fed and threshed, and the elevator or straw pitcher, as it was commonly called, which carried the straw up to the stack. The threshing operation took several workmen, typically the engine driver, the feeder, who fed the sheaves in to the drum, a bond cutter, who cut the string bonds round the sheaves and the bagman, who attended to the bagging of the grain from the drum. Two or three were pitching the sheaves from the corn stack onto the drum, two or three on the straw stack and the man who tended the chaff bags and cleared the waste.

It is inevitable that these machines should first be directed to replace the heaviest and most onerous farming work, by no means to relieve the labourer of their punishing drudgery but more to reduce the landowners reliance upon his workers and thus the costs of labour. As we will see later, this ultimately resulted in mass migration from the land during the nineteenth and early twentieth centuries.

For women working on the land, the farmer's wife and his servants, the introduction of machinery to replace their most burdensome tasks often came much later, almost as an afterthought, although it is true to say that the cumbersome, dirty and heavy steam engines were ill-suited to the more delicate daily tasks such as dairying and the preparation of food.

A dairymaid churning butter from a painting by Millet c.1880. It shows a plunger churn, a type that had been in common use in the medieval period and remnants of such churns have been dated from Roman times. Early references show buttermaking to have been the domain of women, and certainly up to the early twentieth century this remained the case. It was a long and boring task, sometimes taking up to two hours to turn soured cream into butter.

Milking cows, sheep and goats also became work traditionally associated with women on the farm. Before the days of milking parlours, the milkmaid would go out to the fields with her bucket and stool, usually twice a day and taking up to half an hour to milk each cow.

29

The goddess Ceres oversees the work of farm labourers in a woodcut from the fifteenth century. This female figure presided as the harvest deity for well over 2000 years, the lofty position she held contrasts markedly with the woman's actual role in farming which was largely one of subjugation.

Englishman Gervase Markham published The English Huswife, *a handbook for housewives, in 1615 containing 'all the virtuous knowledges and actions both of the mind and body, which ought to be in any complete housewife.' He continues:*

To proceed then to this knowledge of cookery: you shall understand that the first step thereunto is to have knowledge of all sorts of herbs belonging to the kitchen, whether they be for the pot, for salads, for sauces, for serving, or for any other seasoning or adorning. She shall also know the time of the year, month and moon, in which all herbs are to be sown, and when they are in their best flourishing, that gathering all herbs in their height of goodness, she may have the prime use of the same.

Here a seventeenth-century woodcut shows two women at the kitchen table scrubbing pots and pans.

Certainly, until the end of the nineteenth century the traditional work of the farming wife remained much as it always had. Day-to-day duties included the tending of the hearth, furnishing meals for the day (which often meant feeding working men employed on the farm as well as the immediate family), the care of young infants, cleaning the home and attending to the lighting (candles and rush lights in early times, oil lamps later), provision of water in the home and the maintenance of the sanitary arrangements. Making, washing, and mending clothes was also an exclusive role of the housewife. A number of these domestic duties are covered more fully later in this book.

Outside the home the housewife, daughters and women farm servants would be expected to carry out specific duties allied to animal husbandry, the cultivation of crops in the kitchen garden, as well as being called upon to provide additional labour in the fields. In his *Boke of Husbandrie*, published in 1534, Sir Antony Fitzherbert describes the duties expected of a farmer's wife in the sixteenth century:

It is a wyues occupation to wynowe all maner of cornes, to make malte, to wasshe and wrynge, to make heye, shere corne, and in tyme of nede to helpe her husbande to fyll the mucke-wayne or dounge-carte, dryue the ploughe, to loode hey, corne and suche other. And to go or ride to the market, to sel butter, chese, mylke, egges, chekyns, capons, hennes, pygges, gese, and all maner of cornes. And also to bye all maner of necessarye thynges belongynge to houssholde, and to make a trewe rekenynge and acompte to her husbande what she hath payed.

Compare this to the Roman Varro's statement on *Duties of the Housekeeper* included in the previous chapter and we see that, despite the passage of 1500 years, little change has taken place in the home.

On the land it was a man's world so far as the majority of skilled work was concerned, particularly in relation to the use of horses, a male-dominated realm of arcane practices, secret societies and magic. More of this is described in *Goodbye Old Friend: A Sad Farewell to the Working Horse*, a companion to this volume.

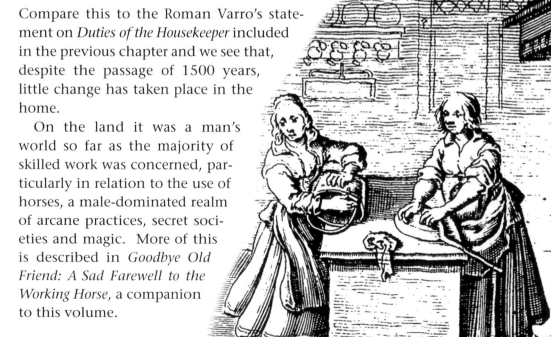

It must again be emphasised that by the nineteenth century there is no 'average' farm from which to draw conclusions regarding the role of women. On large estate farms, the landowner, his wife and family, would have little day-to-day engagement with their labourers who usually lived in tied cottages on the estate and who were under the eye of a bailiff or farm manager. Individual farms of average size would employ live-in farm servants and labourers who shared food and accommodation with the farmer and his wife, while the subsistence farmer and smallholder relied on the immediately family to supply labour, with friends and hired hands brought in to help, particularly at busy times such as harvesting.

The Bickham family c.1885 pose with various relatives and retainers including the cook and their gardener. Though not landowners the family were of farming stock and also acted as bailiffs for the lord of the manor at Bicknoller on the Quantocks, thus were of high standing in the community.

In the spring

How the country people in centuries past must have longed for signs of spring after a hard winter. Food would be running low for both the family and their livestock and the prospect of fresh greenstuff would have been truly mouthwatering after the long months of dearth. Bottled fruit and dried herbs, collected and preserved from the year before, would be almost exhausted, while salt beef and perhaps a smoked ham would have supplemented a meagre winter diet. January and February were known as 'the hungry months' and death from malnutrition was not uncommon among the poorest families even into Queen Victoria's reign.

In the farmyard and in the kitchen garden preparations would begin for the planting of new crops and for the arrival of newborn animals, overseen traditionally by the women. Ewes giving birth in the spring coincided with the beginnings of new

James William Skinner and his wife Sarah with daughter Ada at Seaton, Devon, in 1899, surrounded by domestic pets and poultry and other livestock. Animal husbandry and the cultivation of a small garden to produce food for the family throughout the year was something every working housewife was expected to oversee and regulate, even when live-in servants were on hand.

grass in the meadows while the calving of the house cow and the general herd in spring was favoured as it required less forage to winter a dry cow, and with lush spring grass available in the crucial last weeks of her pregnancy.

Even with stock holding much lower than is to be found on present day farms, the Victorian farmer's wife would find her hands full feeding calves, fostering orphaned lambs and overseeing the successful hatching of chicks, goslings and the like. This on top of her usual daily domestic chores.

In the garden, new ground had to be prepared and seeds sown in order to ensure a healthy crop of vegetables for the summer months, with some to be dried, pickled and bottled for the winter ahead and the surplus possibly for sale in the market.

Away from towns and villages, where access to a market was limited or dependent upon long journeys, farming families first looked to their own resources for most of their food, and hard work undertaken in the spring repaid them handsomely later in the year.

But a woman's work was by no means tied to the home and garden. Labour was at a premium where timing was of the essence regarding sowing and planting, especially in years when variable weather intervened. Again we find specific tasks which appear to have been reserved for woman and children; often the most tedious and repetitive jobs too. According to Henry Stephens who published *The Book of the Farm* in 1844, the employment of women in the planting of the spring potato crop was essential, even quoting a contemporary rhyme to support his reasoning:

Mrs Courtier at Foxworthy Farm in Devon in 1908. She is teaching a calf to feed from a bucket in order to wean it away from its mother.

A smallholding in Edale, Derbyshire with a woman and her young son feeding a flock of ducks. Henry Stephens in The Book of the Farm *notes: 'Ducks begin to lay eggs as early as February so it is possible to obtain an early hatching of ducklings if desired; but early ducklings are not desirable for they do not acquire much flesh.' The management and feeding of fowls, the selection of eggs for hatching and the nurturing of chicks was traditionally an occupation of the women of the farm.*

A dibbling iron.

"— the potato plat
Should now be delved, and with no sparing hand,
The dibbling done, the dropping of the chips,
Is left to little hands, well pleased to lend
Their feeble help: —"

Those 'feeble hands' so patronisingly referred to are those of women and children who were probably not that 'well pleased' to undertake one of the most backbreaking tasks in farming, that of 'dibbling', making holes in the soil in which to drop the seedling potatoes, 'chips' or 'sets'. Prior to this process, Stephens stipulates precise roles for the women workers:

Boys, girls, or women, are required to lead the horse in each cart to and from the dunghill to the part of the field which is receiving the dung. The ploughmen, whose horses are employed in carting the dung, remain at the dunghill, and, assisted by a woman or two, fill the carts with dung as they return empty. One man, the grieve or steward, hawks the dung out of the carts, and gives the land dung in such quantity as is determined on beforehand by the farmer. Three women spread the dung equally in the drills with the small graips [short three-pronged forks], while a fourth goes before and divides it into each drill as it falls in heaps from the carts.

He then conveniently provides an illustration as to how all this should be done:

After the cart has proceeded a few paces, and deposited a few heaps of dung, the foremost of the band of 4 women who spread the dung, divides the heaps with her small common graip into other two heaps one in each of the drills beside her... taking care to remain in her own drill from the one end of the field to the other, shaking to pieces every lump of dung, and teazing out any that may happen to be ranker than the rest, trampling upon the spread dung as she walks along the bottom.

*   The potato planters, after having plenished*

The 'graip' as mentioned by Henry Stephens was a short handled fork used for spreading dung.

their baskets or aprons with sets from the cart upon the headridge, proceed to deposite the sets upon the dung along the drills, at about 8 or 9 inches apart. Some women prefer to carry the sets in coarse aprons instead of baskets, because they are more convenient.

The mind-numbing tedium, the heavy lifting of wet dung and the head-down drudgery of dibbling and planting the length of a field would have been made significantly less appealing in wet weather. Yet this was work that had to be completed and formed part of the yearly round of those involved in farming – a far cry from idealised portraits of rural life made by poets and novelists. Springtime often meant wet, cold weather, heavy soils and mud. Planting potatoes was just one of many such jobs and for the farming wife heavy field work in such conditions often resulted in sickness; possibly a shortened life, certainly a debilitating one where poverty and poor nutrition were spectres always present at the cottage door.

'Dibbling wheat at Hethersett' reads the original caption to this photograph taken c.1910 by Tom Nokes. Note the evident age of the woman on the left.

'The Shepherdess', a typically idealised nineteenth century painting by William-Adolphe Bouguereau (1825–1905). In reality, as farming became more intensive, the management of large flocks of sheep was put into the hands of professional shepherds, with women called in at lambing time to perform the duties of 'lambers'.

The lambing season of Leicester and other heavy breeds of sheep, reared in the arable part of the country, commences about the 11th of March, and continues for about the space of 3 weeks. There is no labour connected with the duties of the shepherd which puts his attention and skill to so severe a test as the lambing season

Henry Stephens thus describes the work of those involved in lambing time, a period vital to the future economy of a farm where sheep were the principal livestock. In 1840 in Suffolk for instance, one out of every hundred agricultural labourers described their occupation as 'shepherd', and while the role was traditionally considered a male occupation, 'lambers', those brought in to help during the lambing season were, and still often are, women. Small hands in delivering difficult births and a natural patience in getting recalcitrant youngsters to feed, are their more natural attributes perhaps.

The docking of lambs' tails, undertaken when they were a few weeks old in order to prevent fly strike and other ailments later in their lives, brought other opportunities for the farming wife, as Ann Hughes described in her diary from 1796:

We did cut the lambs tails yesterday, so today did make pies in my dear mother's way. First we do clean off all the wool, then cut them into little bits and stew them very slow for 20 minnets by the clock, then I do lay some in a deep platter and season with pepper and salt, then a good layer on the top of sliced apples, some chopt parslie, then more tails and apples and parslie till the platter be fulle, then I do put in some of the broth and cover with a good paste, and do cook it in the oven 1 hower and 20 minutes; this be very nice hot or cold.

* * *

The great migration of families from the land into the newly industrialised cities of Britain during the late eighteenth and early nineteenth century, that led to the exploitation of women and children workers among the dark satanic mills, brought labour shortages in farming. The plight of those who remained tied to the land resulted in more burdensome work being heaped on their shoulders, with threats of homelessness pressed on those with tied homes and smallholdings by unscrupulous landowners. The employment of female and child labour expanded significantly in this period, no more so than in the great corn-growing areas of East Anglia where the 'gang system' was introduced. Farmers with a particular piece of work to be done which demanded a large number of labourers, would contract a gangmaster to carry out the work for an agreed sum. The gangmaster would then employ sufficient numbers of women and children to perform the task, working in gangs and paid at a daily rate. This system has modern echoes in the notorious gangmasters who controlled the Chinese labourers who lost their lives in the Morecambe Bay tragedy in 2004.

Tasks performed by both public and private gangs varied according to the season but largely comprised cleaning of land by weeding and stonepicking, and planting and harvesting of root crops such as turnips, potatoes and mangolds. Working from 8am until 5.30pm women were paid typically 8d. or 9d. a day in the mid-nineteenth century, children 3d. or 4d. a day, of which the gangmaster would take up to a third for himself. Some gangs would have to walk in excess of five miles each way to their place of work and if poor weather prevented work they received no pay.

The threat of incarceration in the Poor House, the loss of family and home, drove many to accept their fate at the hands of the gangmasters, while the ambitions of the 'improvers' further encouraged the employment of gangs over local labour:

When I first resided here, the gang-system was not known; the work now done by them was performed by women, or rather it was left undone. But from one or two farmers cultivating their lands in a superior manner, getting their farms perfectly clean and free from weeds; many others have been induced to follow their example and employ more

'The reality of shepherding is revealed in this photograph taken in 1872. Hours were long, working from 6.00am until 6.00pm on around 19 shillings (95p) per week at a time when a shilling would buy two standard 4lb (2kg) loaves.

'The Agricultural Labourer at Home' a some-what fanciful portrayal of rural family life made by the artist H.K. Johnson in 1872, the same date as the photograph above. It does however give some idea of the number of people who would be living together in a modest cottage.

Children were among the greatest to suffer from the impoverishment of the countryside. The care of destitute families fell to the Parish Overseers of the Poor, a position established in the reign of Elizabeth I under which those in need of Poor Relief would be provided with food, clothing and accommodation (often in a workhouse) from a fund drawn on the parish rates. Overseers were replaced in the Poor Law Amendment Act of 1834 with Boards of Guardians and parishes were grouped into unions. This allowed larger centralised workhouses to be built to replace smaller facilities in each parish. Here children of the Union Workhouse at Stoke Abbot in Dorset are paraded before the camera in 1907.

hands; and where there used to be £1 expended in the cultivation of the land 20 years since, there are now £5 expended for the same.

Giving evidence to the 1867 Children's Employment Commission, one observer commented:

...a married women who worked a full day in a gang returned home tired and wearied, and unwilling to make any further exertion to render the cottage comfortable. When the husband returns he finds everything uncomfortable, the cottage dirty, no meal prepared, the children tiresome and quarrelsome, the wife slatternly and cross, and his home so unpleasant to him that he not rarely betakes himself to the public house, and eventually becomes a drunkard. The wife becomes indifferent about her personal appearance, neglectful of her domestic duties, and careless of her children. Those who visit the cottages of the labouring poor will invariably find misery and discomfort in those homes where the wife is employed in field labour, as compared with those where the wife stays at home and attends to her domestic duties.

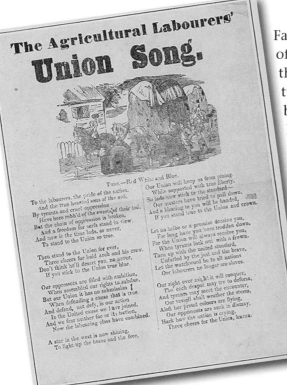

Far from the countryside being a rural idyll so often portrayed by poets, writers and artists of the period, agriculture in the nineteenth century was convulsed by a series of events that brought destitution to thousands. Successive Enclosure Acts were seen by many as the theft of centuries-held rights to cultivate and graze animals on common land, even to build a home there. The Corn Laws, introduced to discourage the importation of cereals from abroad, resulted in bread, the staple of the poor, becoming too expensive for them to buy. The development of lighter and more efficient steam engines and the introduction of machines to replace manual labour witnessed hundreds being thrown out of work, their families mired in poverty.

Social unrest grew. In the 1830s came the Swing Riots in which labourers demanded a minimum wage and tithe and rent reductions. This was the first such mass demonstration by agriculture labourers who took to smashing steam engines and threshing machines. Early attempts to unionise farmworkers ended in activists losing their jobs, being evicted from their homes and, as with the famous Tolpuddle Martyrs, in deportation.

Farmworkers left the land in droves heading for the cities or to new lands overseas. In 1840 20 per cent of the working population was employed in agriculture, falling to 12 per cent by 1880, numbers that are more dramatic when the overall population growth, and consequently the total workforce is taken into account. From 1850 to the end of that century the population of Britain almost doubled, from around 18 million to 32 million.

* * *

In the summer

Even against this turbulent background the necessities of farming meant that age old customs continued. The requirement for labour and the need for women and children workers was never more greatly felt than during the busiest season of the year. In the days before the use of pesticides and automated bird-scaring devices the

A broadside ballad published in 1872 in celebration of the founding of the Union under their leader Joseph Arch. The union was open only to male members. The first lines of the song read:

To the labourers the pride of the nation,
And the true hearted sons of the soil
By tyrants and cruel oppression
Have been robbed of the sweets of their toil.

THE AGRICULTURAL QUESTION SETTLED.

In this cartoon from 1845 the Prime Ministers turns his back on a starving farm labourer, his wife and children with the words 'I'm very sorry my good man, but I can do nothing for you.'

39

'The Bird Scarer' by William Knight Keeling (1807–1886). The boy holds in his hand a wooden rattle that, when revolved would make a loud 'clacking' sound to drive off birds. Women and children were often left to take on such work as men refused to do it as being tedious or wasteful of their skills.

encroachment of weeds into a crop and the depredation by flocks of birds of newly sown seed and young plants was a serious issue for farmers. Bird scaring was a job more often left to boys and girls who, armed with various types of bird scarer, would sit all day in the fields driving rooks, pigeons and other vermin away. Men refused to take on this work, but women earned additional monies by doing so, a point made by Norfolk farmer Thomas Hudson, writing in the 1860s:

The work done by them [women] is of great importance, both to the support of their families, and to the land. There are no manufactories here, and consequently a poor man with barely sufficient earnings for himself and wife could not possibly maintain a family of four or five grown-up daughters, and the work performed by the women and girls could not, or at any rate would not in fact, ever be done by men. I do not see any other way in which their work, e.g., weeding etc., could be done.

In her paper 'Field-Faring Women' (1993), Karen Sayer reinforces the suggestion that the burden of laborious field work fell upon the shoulders of women and that Victorian sensibilities condemned those who were obliged to take on such work as unsexed and immoral. The upper classes had always considered manual labour as vulgar, more so if women were thus engaged, and the newly risen middle classes adopted this attitude with relish. For others it was more a matter of a fair day's pay than social stigma as reported in an East Anglian newspaper in 1867:

The French Revolution at the end of the eighteenth century politicised art in Europe for decades. At the time Courbet completed this painting in the late 1840s Europe was undergoing two years of poor harvest leading to hunger and starvation among the peasantry. 1848 became known as The Year of Revolution with a series of upheavals springing up throughout Europe. In this painting 'The Young Women from the Village', the artist shows a group of wealthy young ladies giving alms to a young peasant girl they have encountered upon their walk. Richly dressed, their pose, and the title of the painting itself, reflects the prevailing patronising attitude of the wealthy to the rural poor throughout Europe.

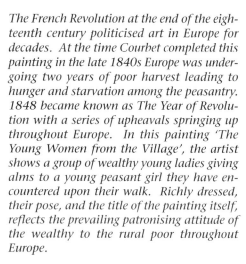

Farmers may talk at their monthly meetings about labour being well remunerated; conservative journals may comment on, and lament over, the evils of the gang system practised in the fens of Lincolnshire; but will the public believe them? Is 1s 6d per day a fair remuneration for a woman to toil in the fields and unsex herself?

But just as their male counterparts were organising their labour in order to resist the worst excesses of landowners, so groups of women not only supported the men, in some cases they took direct action themselves. In 1873 the *Fife Herald* reported:

STRIKE AMONG FEMALE OUT-DOOR WORKERS
The females employed on a farm in this district have been out on strike for several days past, on a question of wages. They have been paid 1s 2d a day, but demand an advance, which, as yet, has not been complied with.

Before machines, the success of the grain harvest, always at the mercy of the weather, was dependent upon having the hands available to cut the standing fields of corn, gather and stand the stooks to dry them, and finally to convey all to the barns and ricks ready for threshing later in the year. As mentioned earlier, the tradition of gleaning was held to be an almost exclusively female role and is often portrayed romantically by writers and authors.

Though not subject to so great a degree to the vagaries of rainfall, the hay harvest brought similar demands to farming communities; there could never be too many hands to help even after the introduction of horse-drawn reapers and binders.

PRIZE PEASANT   **RIVALS**   PRIZE PIG

Cartoon illustrating the poverty of Victorian farm labourers, suggesting they were considered lower than livestock by the landowners. If the welfare of male workers was held so cheap then the plight of women working on the land was far worse.

The romanticisation of rural life by Victorian artists is exemplified in 'Recalling the Gleaners from the Fields', an 1858 painting by Jules Breton. It portrays a youth calling to the women who have been labouring until the light fades from the evening sky.

41

A love-token favour made from barley straw.

Peter De Wint's painting 'Harvesters Resting' c.1820 captures the quiet community of harvest time in the pre-industrialised age of farming.

Customs associated with the centuries-old traditions of harvest had already begun to fade by the time Victoria took the throne in 1837. Pagan festivals at their core many, if practised at all, are nowadays annual events maintained or revived simply for fun. Others, later absorbed by Christianity, survive in the form of harvest festivals, although the modern incarnation of this was begun in 1843 by the Revd Robert Hawker of Morwenstow in Cornwall when he invited parishioners to join in thanksgiving for the harvest. It is from this time that hymns such as 'We Plough the Fields and Scatter' became popular.

Much earlier customs, such as Crying the Neck and the making of corn dollies celebrated harvest in a more visceral way and in which the success of planting, reaping and winnowing was bound up in a belief in gods and goddesses of the harvest. Men and women would fashion corn dollies as love-tokens for sweethearts. Known as harvest knots these were worn as a buttonhole and, according to tradition, such a favour given by a man or boy to a female would still have its ears of corn attached. Those tokens given by a woman or girl to a man would have been made of straw with the ears of corn removed; the grain being the (male) seed of new life from which the future crop is born, the (female) soil being 'mother earth', the bearer of new life in imitation of women being the bearers of children.

THE TURN OF THE YEAR

The horse-drawn reaper, introduced in the 1830s, was the first machine to intrude significantly upon what had previously been a process done entirely by hand. This cut the crop close to the ground leaving hay or grain lying in rows from where it was gathered up by hand. In the late 1870s the self-binder replaced most of the handwork of the harvest field, cutting and binding sheaves in one operation and thus replacing the mowing gangs who previously scythed the crop, drastically reducing the numbers of labourers required to gather it in. Within a few years small steam tractors began to take the place of horses and the quiet of the harvest fields redolent of centuries

In parts of the country more remote from industrialised centres, on small farms not conducive to large-scale production, subsistence farming and its age-old traditions continued well into the twentieth century. Here, on a Dartmoor farm c. 1886, Annie Huxtable has brought food and a kettle of tea out to the workers, George Ellis, Mr Nichols and John and George Derges. They are building a hay rick, their pitchforks standing beside them, and hand made wooden rakes rest on the hedge behind.

Faced by rising labour costs brought on in part by the movement of farmworkers to the cities, landowners sought to find a solution through the use of machines. Nineteenth-century manufacturers devised numerous steam-powered engines aimed at replacing manpower. Here a group of landowners watch the trial of an engine designed to cultivate new ground. Mechanical breakdowns, initial cost and the sheer weight of such machines that became bogged down on soft soil doomed many to failure. But the future of all those who worked in farming was inexorably changing.

past, broken only by the voices of the labourers as they worked, now rang to the clatter of machinery, the summer sky clouded by smoke and steam.

While there was much variation across the country, in areas traditionally given over to arable crops the demand for food from the growing cities increased landowners' interest in producing cash crops such a vegetables to feed the urban population. Migration from the land to the cities drove up agricultural wages. A contemporary commentator, Thomas Barnes, in 1859 wrote 'a man of agricultural class considered himself well paid and a big wage if he got ten or twelve shillings for his week's wage'.' By 1870 wages for labourers on the land rose to 16 shillings per week and, for a time, those who remained working on the land enjoyed better times, although the work they were called upon to do grew no less demanding. Immigrant labour, principally from Ireland, to a degree alleviated the labour shortage and helped keep wages stable but the overall effect was to encourage landowners to seek more feverishly mechanical means by which many of the farming tasks might now be more cheaply undertaken.

By the end of Victoria's reign in the early years of the twentieth century reaper-binders were a common sight in the cornfields of Britain. And while steam and oil-powered tractors were beginning to replace horse-power, the majority of farms still relied on horses. Here, on a farm near Crediton in Devon, women and children are stooking sheaves of corn that have come off the back of the horse-drawn binder.

In the autumn and winter

In past centuries autumn was the season in which the skills of the farming wife would be called upon to ensure the survival of her family through the winter and into the following spring. A poor summer's harvest and a wet autumn would mean meagre rations for the farm stock that had to be kept alive through the winter which in turn would mean short rations for the family. A kind summer with warm weather extending through September and into October provided the bounty to see the family through, but only by the knowledge and hard work of the farming wife would this be stored and preserved to last the coming months. It was also at this time that the sowing and tending of the cottage garden in spring, weeding and watering during summer, literally bore fruit.

From the seventeenth century writers had increasingly turned their hand to instructions on how the good housewife should order and maintain her home and family. Prominent among these was Hannah Wolley (1622–c.1675) who was probably the first woman to earn a living from her publications on household management. Among her works is the succinctly titled *The Queen-like Closet or Rich Cabinet Stored With All Manner Of Rare Receipts For Preserving, Candying and Cookery. Very Pleasant And Beneficial To All Ingenious Persons Of The Female Sex.* Her 'receipts' range widely from the preservation of gooseberries, the drying of pears and other fruit, the candying of carrots, and the 'stretching of sheeps guts'.

Hannah Wolley the seventeenth century writer whose recipes included a cure for consumption involving a liquor made from snails and crushed sugar 'to be taken morning and evening a spoonful at a time.'

Isabella Mary Beeton (1836–1865), the First Lady of cookery books. The Book of House-hold Management *sold 60 000 copies in its first year of publication in 1861 and by the end of that decade two million had been sold.*

A century later, in 1732, Richard Bradley's *The Country Housewife and Lady's Director In the Management of a House, and the Delights and Profits of a Farm* appears on the scene, in the introduction to which the author writes:

The Reason which induces me to address the following Piece to the Fair Sex, is, because the principal Matters contained in it are within the Liberty of their Province. The Art of Oeconomy is divided... between the Men and the Women; the Men have the most dangerous and laborious Share of it in the Fields, and without doors, and the Women have the Care and Management of every Business within doors, and to see after the good ordering of whatever is belonging to the House.

This reinforcement of the male role as being one of hard labour while the 'fair sex' looks after the home is significant as, by ignoring the poverty of the poorest in society where women are obliged to labour alongside men in the fields, these writers are addressing an emerging class who warm to the distinction that they are 'different', that they have time to order their households in a civilised manner and, not only that, also that they can read.

By the time Mrs Beeton's famous *Book of Household Management* is published in 1861, this middle class has secured a firm place in the social strata, and not only does the mid Victorian housewife have access to a wide range of comestibles from which to prepare sumptuous meals, she now has servants to help her.

Between 1830 and 1860 Britain's rail network grew from less than 100 miles to over 10 000 miles. The economic and social effects of this on previously remote rural areas was dramatic. Here a broad gauge locomotive stands at Watchet station in 1867, five years after the railway was opened to this north Devon harbour town. Hundreds of similar stations and railway halts through Britain allowed fast transport of milk, meat, fish, fruit and vegetables from the countryside to the cities. Livestock could now be transported in large numbers over great distances to feed the population of the industrialised centres. In return those living in the countryside could order and receive goods made in the cities.

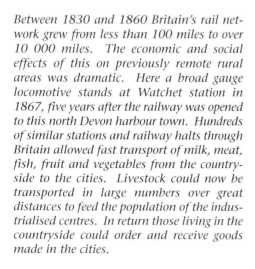

THE TURN OF THE YEAR

Improvements to the road network and the expansion of railways made the ingredients called for in these comprehensive recipe books readily available to town dwellers, with grocers, greengrocers, dairymen, fishmongers, butchers and bakers shops springing up in every Victorian high street.

*   *   *

Such facilities were few and far between in the countryside and, anyway, middle class aspirations seeped more slowly into the lives of those who lived away from urban centres, the farming community in particular taking a stubborn pride in hanging on to tradition and with whom thriftiness remained a cardinal virtue. In rural areas, where shops were few and goods less easily obtained, make-do-and-mend and self-sufficiency in food, for the time being, remained the watchword

Strawberry pickers in the Hampshire countryside in the first years of the twentieth century. The picking itself was largely left to women and children who filled baskets made of poplar wood in which the fruit was transported. In the background a train stands at Swanwick Station waiting to take the strawberries on to urban markets.

The carrier's cart became an increasingly familiar sight on rural roads as railways created supply and demand for produce both in urban and rural areas. The carrier provided a link between the railway stations and the outlying communities delivering orders taken on the previous trip. Daily deliveries of milk, bread and other perishables also grew as country people moved away from self-sufficiency. Here, Samuel Stenner and his daughter Vera deliver groceries to the Ship Inn at Porlock c.1910.

WALTER SHAW & Co

16 & 17, Park Street, BIRMINGHAM.

New Prize Medal Cooking Range.

Has bottom heat to oven and will bake bread.

Saves 50 per cent. in fuel.

Has Patent rising bottom to reduce fire.

The vast manufactories of Birmingham and the North created markets for their products through extensive advertising. Housewives were persuaded to adopt new-fangled appliances for the home as in this 'Prize Medal Range' shown in a catalogue from 1894.

Invented in 1855, linoleum was considered a boon to those living in old farmhouses and cottages with stone, slate or lime-ash floors. Here was a cheap product that was easily swept and cleaned and, after all, cleanliness is next to godliness.

The transport revolution was a boon to those farmers whose land was suited to producing crops or livestock on a large scale. The public developed a taste for seasonal fruit and vegetables and more sophisticated city dwellers now desired country flowers to brighten their homes.

The mixed farming economy that had been the staple of so many small farms now, with a guaranteed market, moved towards specialism, and consequently farms began to grow in size at the same time as increasing mechanisation reduced the need for permanent labour.

And just as the railway transported produce to the towns so it brought 'modern' manufactured goods, the subject of bright and tempting advertisements, to the countryside. This led to an increase in the number of carriers who, on their weekly rounds, delivered ordered goods to the housewife's door: new cleaning products, linoleum and lamp oil to brighten hearth and home.

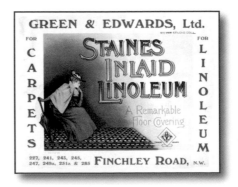

GREEN & EDWARDS, Ltd.

FOR CARPETS

STAINES INLAID LINOLEUM A Remarkable Floor Covering

FOR LINOLEUM

227, 241, 243, 245, 247, 249a, 251a & 285 FINCHLEY ROAD, N.W.

Hearth and Home

"Of all those acquirements, which more particularly belong to the feminine character, there are none which take a higher rank, in our estimation, than such as enter into a knowledge of household duties; for on these are perpetually dependent the happiness, comfort, and well-being of a family."

Mrs Beeton's *Book of Household Management*

There is no such thing as a typical farmhouse or cottage. The period in which they were first constructed, the prevailing economy, the materials available and the local traditions of building styles all play a part in how they look. No two buildings are exactly the same and many have been restyled, extended and rebuilt over the centuries often changing their appearance completely. For the purpose of this chapter we will attempt to form an amalgam approximating to a typical home found in late nineteenth and early twentieth century.

Four very different farmhouses demonstrate the range of design and materials used in their construction. Clockwise from top left: 1. Hemyock Castle Farm, Devon, seen in 1920, built in part from local chert stone. Note the thatched roof. 2. Gaterounds Farm near Newdigate in Surrey dates from the sixteenth century and is constructed on a timber frame with brick infill and with a tiled roof. 3. Brick-built Locks Farm, Newton on the Isle of Wight, rests on Norman foundations and has undergone extensive restoration and rebuilding over the centuries. 4. Woodlands Manor is a grand house dating from the fourteenth century and only became a farmhouse in the mid 1700s. Now Grade I listed it is built from local limestone and when this photograph was taken, in the late 1800s, it had a stone slate roof.

As with farmhouses, no two cottages were the same and many had their origins in far simpler dwellings than those that stand on the same site today. Clockwise from top left: 1. Jolly Lane Cot is a thatched Dartmoor cottage, seen here in 1889. It is said to have been 'built in a day' under a local law that declared that a man could claim the house and land on which his dwelling stood if he could have it built and roofed with a fire in the hearth between sunrise and sunset. 2. Two tiny cottage with tiled roofs sit side-by-side in Narborough, Norfolk. In the early 1900s this was the home of a local coachman. 3. The cottager and her cat stand outside a thatched cottage with limewashed walls at Elmsett in Suffolk in the 1920s. 4. Part of this cob-walled cottage on Hayling Island, Hampshire, looks in danger of collapse through lack of maintenance. Its roof part-tiled and part-thatched, an ivy-clad end wall has had much of the clay and straw cob washed-away. Many such rural cottages simply fell into ruin during the nineteenth century as people left the countryside for the cities.

A mother with her child at a cottage doorway, Stiniel near Chagford, Devon in 1895.

As far as the farmer's and cottager's wife was concerned contemporary writers, and indeed the monarch herself, left women in no doubt of their role. In the decades towards the end of Queen Victoria's reign bookseller's shelves were weighed down with volume on volume of practical guidance for housewives and mothers. Much of this information was linked to the tenets of the Christian religion and to the popularity of non-conformist faiths among the working classes extolling, among others, the virtues of hard work, moral continence (especially where sex was concerned) and teetotalism. As late as 1910, the writings of Marion Mills Miller, author of *Practical Suggestions for Mother and Housewife*, typify the style:

What a tribute to the worth of woman are the names by which she is enshrined in common speech! What tender associations halo the names of wife, mother, sister and daughter! It must never be forgotten that the dearest, most sacred of these names, are, in origin, connected with the dignity of service. In early speech the wife, or wife-man (woman) was the 'weaver,' whose care it was to clothe the family, as it was the husband's duty to 'feed' it, or to provide the materials of sustenance. The mother or matron was named from the most tender and sacred of human functions, the nursing of the babe; the daughter from her original duty, in the pastoral age, of milking the cows.

Left: Grampound and Creed Mothers' Union meet in Creed rectory Garden in 1895. The organisation was founded by Mary Sumner in 1876 who was inspired to start the movement after the birth of her first grandchild. Remembering her own difficulties when she first became a mother, Sumner wanted to bring mothers of all social classes together to provide support for one another.

Above: A pledge card for membership of The Band of Hope signed in 1886. 'Signing the Pledge' was a principal feature of this Temperance organisation whose members swore to abstain from drinking alcohol. Originally proposed by a Baptist minister, Jabez Tunnicliff, in 1847, the organisation became national in 1885, holding marches and rallies against the evils of drink. The Band of Hope and similar societies were primarily working class movements and were tied in with both religious renewal and progressive politics, particularly female suffrage.

These years saw what was the beginning of female crusading embodied in the proliferation of women's organisations aimed at maintaining the traditions of motherhood, albeit under the authority of the husband. This was the seedbed from which the demands for equality for women flowered. As early as 1866 John Stuart Mill MP proposed an amendment to the 1866 Reform Bill calling for the inclusion of women on the same terms as men. In 1882 The Married Women's Property Act became law; a pivotal point in that for the first time it allowed married women to own and control their own property.

Newspapers and books gave a national voice to political and literary reformers while the wealth of the Empire brought financial independence to many families whose lives had previously been held in fealty to the landowning classes. Science began to dilute the influence that religion had previously exercised over the lower classes and socialism appeared as a viable alternative to the established order. By 1903, the suffrage campaign entered a new phase with the formation of the Women's Social and Political Union by Emmeline Pankhurst.

For most, the social revolution was not a thing they were consciously engaged upon, more something that simply happened to them; and perhaps resistance to change has always been deliberate among rural communities. Nonetheless, earlier in the century William Cobbett, farmer and journalist, was propounding his radical ideas aimed specifically at the farm labourer and his family. In his *Cottage Economy*, published in 1822, he foresees the improvements that social change will bring about:

> *Better times, however, are approaching. The labourer now appears likely to obtain that hire of which he is worthy; and, therefore, this appears to me to be the time to press upon him the duty of using his best exertions for the rearing of his family in a manner that must give him the best security for happiness to himself, his wife and children, and to make him, in all respects, what his forefathers were. The people of England have been famed, in all ages, for their good living; for the abundance of their food and goodness of their attire. The old sayings about English roast beef and plum-pudding, and about English hospitality, had not their foundation in nothing.*

*   *   *

A fireplace in a Scottish croft c.1900. Note the plunger churn on the left.

Opposite is a composite drawing of a country cottage at around the turn of the century which first appeared in *The Old Devon Farmhouse* by Peter Brears. While the arrangement of this cross passage dwelling is typical of the Westcountry, what we find in the interior is not atypical of rural dwellings found throughout the country. The plan of the original building dates from the medieval period, albeit somewhat superior to the labourer's cottage. Gone is the austere functionality of earlier centuries, now displaced by arrays of purely decorative object d'art; the little tripod table draped with a tasseled cloth and bearing a glass-domed display of waxed flowers, the mantlepiece crowded with porcelain figures, the walls hung with paintings. Yet here among the bric-a-brac so beloved of the Victorians there remain furnishings and utensils that date back centuries: the oak and ash bench in the back kitchen, the table laden with earthen jugs and pots, the curved settles and the eighteenth century windsor chairs.

Most redolent of the dwelling's origins is the open fireplace with its bread oven and array of pot hooks, chimney cranes, hangers, trivets and dogs. In front of the fire sits a roasting jack. Yet these venerable accoutrements of the hearth, the age-old heart of the home, the provider of both heat and food, would be considered old-fashioned as Victoria's reign reached its close, and by Edwardian times even in the poorest of households almost all of this would be swept away. It has to be said that whatever the success of Cobbett's and his fellow social reformers' call for the farm labourer and his wife to wake up to change, the introduction of the humble kitchen range played a significant role in actually making that change happen.

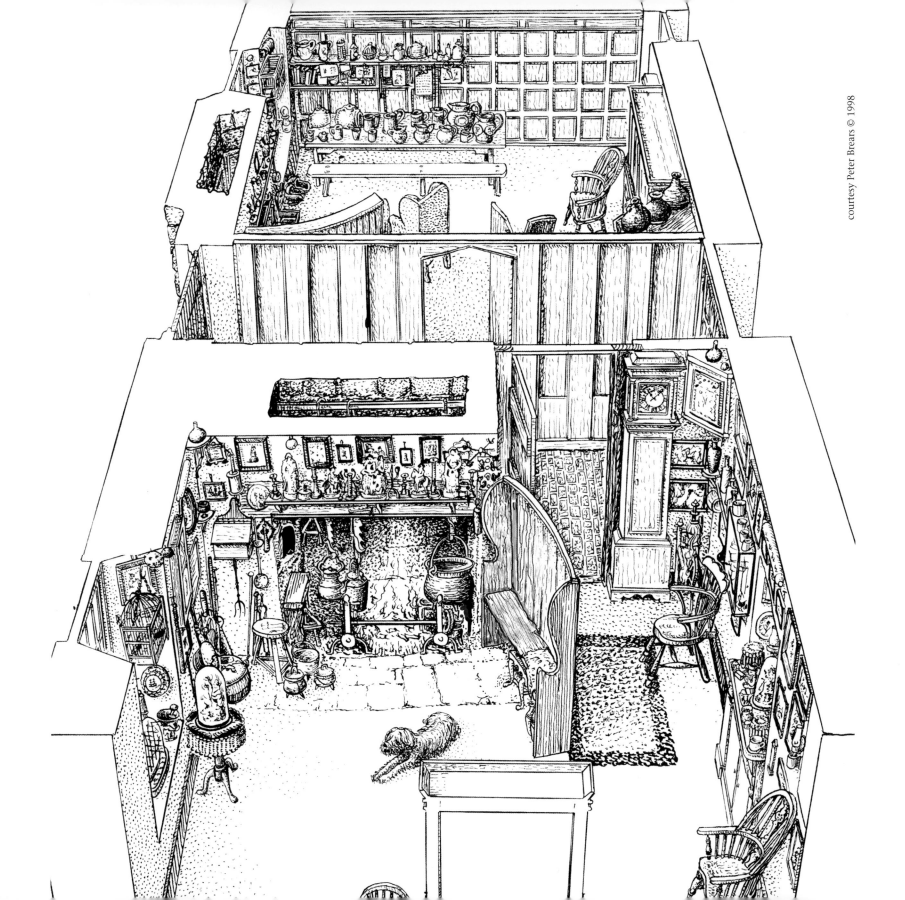

The fireplace in a Dartmoor cottage from around 1900. Pot hooks hang from the chimney supporting a stewpan and a preserving pan. The grime of years colours the lime-washed walls and, in the winter months particularly the smell of smoke pervaded the cottagers' clothes.

In *Sketches of the Bucks Countryside*, published in 1934, the author recalls a similar cottage to that depicted by Peter Brears as it appeared at the turn of the century:

It was one of those cottage rooms that contain a wide open fireplace left in its original state; but the dog irons had given place to a kitchen range backed close to the wall, and the spacious chimney was almost blocked by a large piece of tin placed on the riddy-hole from which the pot hooks and hanger still hung, yet leaving sufficient vent for the smoke to freely ascend. As in most old cottages, the ceiling was low and supported by a transverse beam, the long mantleshelf was crowded with old china and various ornaments of a bygone generation, and on the opposite wall ticked an old-fashioned clock.

The open hearth with its constantly glowing fire was not simply the practical centre of home life, its presence pervaded the very being of farming families and labourers, filling the home with dust, darkening their skin and suffusing their clothes with an ever-present bouquet of smoke. It was one of the woman's daily chores to mitigate the effects of this grime as a Suffolk housewife recalls:

The kitchen had a copper which always smoked so that the door had to be left open even in the winter to let out the smoke. There was an open fireplace with a white chalked hearthstone which had to be cleaned every day with chalk which was brought from the downs... In the front room there was coconut matting on the floor which we children had to take to the orchard every Saturday and pull over the grass to clean it; once the floor was swept and washed it was brought in again.

Farmhouses were generally larger than cottages, not only due to the relative wealth of the owners but to accommodate 'live-in' farm labourers and other servants who shared meals with the farmer and his family. In some parts of the country the traditional farmhouse also accommodated space for the animals, a practical solution in keeping everything under one roof especially in winter and, ignoring the odours, with the additional benefit of the warmth of the animals providing extra heat.

An open fireplace in a cottage in Porlock Somerset c.1910. Note the wallpaper, also the lace mantleshelf flounce, a decorative touch in such a modest home and typical of the gentrification that went on in the late Victorian period.

This fanciful painting 'The New Arrival' by artist Carlton Alfred Smith (1853–1946) nonetheless contains all the elements to be found in a Victorian cottage kitchen: the open hearth, brick floor, simple furnishing and everyday utensils.

A photograph dated 1892 of Higher Merripit farm, a Dartmoor longhouse combining accommodation both for the family and for livestock all under one roof. In this instance the roof is thatched as was commonplace on dwellings where suitable stone or slate was unavailable – and in any case thatch was the material of choice for many, it being readily available, cheap, easy to replace and providing excellent insulation.

Inset: Farmer and Mrs Cleeve and their daughter at Higher Merripit, 1892.

This single-dwelling arrangement in which part of the structure provided accommodation for livestock alongside the family was by no means confined to the Westcountry and similar farmsteads can be found throughout Britain. In his book *The Cottages and Village Life of Rural England* the historian P.H. Ditchfield describes one such farm in the Yorkshire Dales:

Some Dalesmen's houses have the dwelling house, barn or stables or cowhouse all under one roof. In the centre is the barn or threshing-floor, with a large pair of folding doors

at one end and a small winnowing door at the other. On one side is the dwelling-house and on the other the stables or ox-house. Sometimes the central part was a sort of passage with doors leading on one side to the habitation of the family, and the other to that of the animals, together with a barn. The reason why we call the entrance to a house the threshold is because the threshing floor was placed there. In the Dalesman's house he used to feed not only his family, but his labourers, who arranged themselves according to seniority at a long table remote from the fire, while he and his family sat at a round table near the hearth.

Artists continued to romanticise rural life, even the drudgery of doing the laundry, as portrayed in this postcard from the 'Oilette' series which was introduced in 1903. Washing clothes was usually done in the open air until the wash house became commonplace from the early 1800s. These buildings, either standing alone or sometimes built on to existing dwellings, contained a 'copper', a large inverted bell-shaped vessel built into a brick surround containing a fire hole for heating the water. In wet weather the wash house also provided a place to dry clothes.

WASHING DAY IN THE HIGHLANDS.

Pears Soap is said to be the world's first and oldest brand name and Thomas Barratt, manager of the firm in the mid 1800s is credited with being the father of modern advertising, using contemporary artists to create images through which to promote and sell his products.

The rural housewife of the late 1800s and early 1900s, while lacking the instant access to goods and services enjoyed by her urban counterparts, nonetheless found many opportunities for improving her life. In the home, as on the land, this was an age of innovation and invention, and for almost the first time manufacturers were targeting women with an array of labourer saving devices. The two major domestic duties, that of cooking and cleaning, had for centuries changed little so far as the apparatus and utensils used were concerned. Even late into the nineteenth century washing of clothes took place in a communal wash house, or even at the riverbank, lye (a mixture of urine and ash to produce a strong alkali) being used as a cleaning agent until soap (made from animal fat and lye) came into common use from the eighteenth century onwards.

Andrew Pears produced his cosmetic soap in the early 1800s, basing his product on glycerine to produce a much gentler lather. In 1884 Lever Brothers introduced the first packaged and branded laundry soap and four years later the Johnson Soap Company introduced Palmolive soap, using palm and olive oils which made them more suited to washing the person. By 1900 Palmolive became the world's bestselling soap. Furious competition arose between the soap manufacturers, each producing advertisements aimed at the housewife and often equating cleanliness with moral purity. The country housewife was also now able to purchase her soap from the local carrier, or from the increasing number of village shops.

Cooking was transformed too; the open fires, iron pots and fire-irons of earlier centuries now rapidly being replaced by cast-iron kitchen ranges designed to fit neatly into the original fireplace openings and using existing chimneys. These stoves, fuelled by wood, coal and coal oil and offering a relatively clean and instant heat, transformed the farmhouse and cottage kitchen, heralding in a new era of 'scientific cookery'.

Not only was the housewife expected to produce simple daily sustenance for her husband and family – just as she was responsible for effecting the 'goodness' that came from cleanliness – she was now called upon to embrace the virtues of producing 'good' food, as described later in this book.

Edward Mott's shop in Markyate, Herts, photographed c.1900. The expansion of the railways brought everyday goods into the reach of most parts of the countryside and village shops sprang up in most communities, many simply taking over a spare room in a cottage. Their owners stocked a wide range of household goods though not all, as in Mr Mott's case, framed art prints and sculpture alongside tea, vegetables and paintbrushes.

Elizabeth Johns of Veryan, cat on her knee, sits beside her Cornish range c.1900. This was a coal-fired version as can be seen from the scuttle on the floor.

Manufacturers vied with each other in attracting the attention of the housewife to their particular model of cooking range, usually claiming a unique feature that made their equipment better than the next. Regional variations also existed, complying to the traditional methods of cooking and local dishes. The Cornish range for instance, that first appeared around 1840, took into account the baking of pasties and the scalding of clotted cream. The range had an adjustable plate or pan rack, dampers to control the heat, an easily removable ash-tray (the ashes would be emptied into a metal bucket and kept for tipping down the privy) and removable iron rings of varying sizes in the 'slab' above the fire that allowed a faster boil or slower simmer.

A Lincolnshire countryman, writing about his Edwardian childhood, recalls the versatility of such ranges:

The kitchen was fitted with a cast-iron range. The oven sat on one side of the fire and the boiler for heating the water on the other. The were a few different types of ranges but the principles were the same. My father prepared his fire-lighting material each

Technological innovation in the home transformed the working lives of all those involved in domestic work, not least the growing number of those employed as domestic servants in the late Victorian period. Here two housemaids and a cook pose alongside the gardener employed at Carclew House in Cornwall c.1900. Each woman holds an item denoting their duties, a sewing machine, a tea pot and a rolling pin.

By 1900 there were over 1.7 million women employed in domestic service, a rise of over a million from fifty years earlier. This was in part due to the decline of women engaged in agriculture who now, as part of the economic boom in the later years of Victoria's reign found themselves in demand by families employing live-in maids, cooks etc. Women in service represented about 35 per cent of the working adult population compared to less than 1 per cent of men so engaged.

weekend. He made up a bundle of different sizes of sticks for each day of the week. Arising between 5.30 and 6.00am he would clear out the ashes from the previous day, put some paper in the bottom of the grate, then lay the sticks, small ones at the bottom and the larger pieces at the top. Next he placed a filled kettle on the top of the sticks and put pieces of coal round the kettle and lit the paper. By this time the kettle was boiling and the coal burning but all the sticks had gone. When the kettle was removed the fire was going well and the breakfast was ready. Some women hung a short metal shelf on the bars of the grate; this enable them to put a flat iron near the fire. When the iron was hot enough, a second iron was put to the heat and in this way the ironing was done. My mother used to put her irons in the hot oven; she said the face of the iron kept much smoother than way.

An added advantage was that the cast-iron casing of these stoves also produced radiated heat that kept the kitchen warm throughout the year.

Along with stoves came an avalanche of other kitchen appliances aimed at taking the drudgery out of the housewife's domestic chores. Pots and pans no longer subjected to the flames of an open fire could be made of lighter materials. Instead of large stewpots bubbling away for days, food could be conveniently cooked to provide individual meals. Furnishing too became more refined, rough hewn benches and tables being replaced by factory-made furniture. Wallpaper became fashionable, though impracticable on the rough whitewashed walls of many homes.

The kitchen range with its built-in water boiler brought the task of washing clothes into the labourer's home for the first time. Hitherto, clothes were washed only occasionally, if at all, and usually in the open air or in a separate wash house, and ironing was unheard of among the poor.

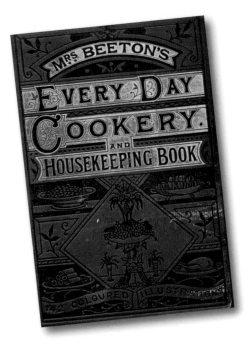

Mrs Beeton's Book of Household Managment *spawned whole libraries of similar works aimed at the 'modern' housewife. Isabella Mary Beeton herself produced a number of spin-off titles such as* Everyday Cookery.

Lighting the home also improved, rush lights, candles and other primitive methods giving way to oil lamps, gas mantles and electricity, although for many living on farms and in villages, gas and electricity supplies were a long time coming.

The popularity of Mrs Beeton's cookery books led to a flood of others and by the early 1900s the image beloved by advertisers and publishers (even today) of the housewife as a domestic goddess, while yet in its infancy, was slumbering happily in the nursery. With improvements in printing technology books became cheaper, opening up a new market to people who hitherto could afford only newspapers. Public libraries further expanded readership encouraging publishers to diversify to meet more specialist needs. Invalid cookery already formed a section in many general cookery books; now separate volumes were devoted to this subject.

And yet with all this, the country wife maintained traditions of cooking and cleaning well after the time that it had been generally abandoned elsewhere. The strong influence of the seasonal activities in farming and how and when this affected what food was available, mitigated the dictates of fashion and change. A writer recalling his Edwardian youth remembers:

We had none of those contrivances which are now regarded as essential. No electricity. No telephone. No running water. No toilet or bathroom. Only washbasins and chamberpots. Look with your mind's eye at the house where I was born. It was 400 years old, built of oak beams filled in with wattle and daub. The kitchen range was fired by coal. All our water was drawn from the well. Each day presented 'the trivial round, the common task'. Pump up the water. Fill the buckets and kettles. Get in the wood and coal. See to the oil lamp. Make ready the candlesticks. Go to the W.C. It was outside at the end of the garden. But we were happy for all that. Our forerunners had lived in this way for centuries.

In the following chapters we look at the 'trivial round, the common task' of the farmer's wife from the Victorian period forward.

The Dairymaid

Under a daisied bank
There stands a rich red ruminating cow,
And hard against her flank
A cotton-hooded milkmaid bends her brow.
                    'The Milkmaid' Thomas Hardy

O f all the traditional occupations in farming, none is so directly related to women than that of dairying. While stockmen, male cowherds and dairymen were also widely engaged, and in greater numbers, caring for young cattle and the production of milk, butter, cream and cheese is a feminine role. Indeed, so rooted in folklore and

John Savage's amusing etching of Marcellus Laroon's 'The Merry Milk Maid' (c.1688) depicts a young woman selling milk in the street carrying a huge array of vessels on her head.

'Milk for the Calves' by Frederick Morgan, 1883, portrays a dairymaid feeding the young animals that have been weaned from their mother and yet require their daily intake of milk. Many Victorian painters used such rural scenes as allegories portraying mother-hood.

'The Dairymaid', 1879 by the artist Mansel Lewis (1845–1931). It was once usual for cows to be milked in the fields where they were grazing rather than calling them in to the farmyard to be milked. This required a good deal of skill and patience on the part of the milkmaid, as anyone who has worked with cattle will know. Here the elderly dairymaid, three-legged milking stool under one arm and her milk bucket in hand, returns from the herd.

popular literature is this role that the milkmaid became inextricably linked with attributes of fecundity and sexuality. In 'Two Gentlemen of Verona' Shakespeare's character Launce declaims:

> *...yet 'tis a woman; but what woman, I*
> *will not tell myself; and yet 'tis a milkmaid; yet*
> *'tis not a maid, for she hath had gossips; yet 'tis*
> *a maid, for she is her master's maid, and serves for*
> *wages.*

The lines are full of innuendo, well understood by the play's sixteenth-century audience, implying the 'maid' cannot be a 'maid', while her 'serving for wages' has a clear double meaning. The very act of milking by hand and other duties of dairymaids has provided bawdy folksong writers with endless lewd insinuations, as in the opening verse of the seventeenth-century 'Two Maidens Went Milking':

> *Two maidens went milking one day*
> *And the wind it did blow high*
> *And the wind it did blow low*
> *And it toss-ed their pails to and fro, la, la, la*
> *And it toss-ed their pails to and fro.*

...and three centuries later to Laurie Lee's beautiful poem 'Milkmaid' and the line 'the girl dreams milk within her body's field'.

In *The Romantic Adventures of a Milkmaid*, published in 1883, Thomas Hardy employed the milkmaid to portray a character whose naiveté would be instantly familiar to his readers; a girl whose silly romantic dreams are easily forgiven. In the better known *Tess of the d'Urbervilles*, Hardy's heroine also works as a dairymaid.

In truth the work of the dairymaid required skill in dealing with large animals, working long hours in every kind of weather. Milking cows in a byre is a relatively recent development brought about with the introduction of milking machines and the farming of large dairy herds. Before then most farms kept only a small number of cows, the size of the herd dictated by the amount of winter fodder the farmer could expect to grow. In Gloucestershire for instance, a county known for its dairy cattle, the agriculturalist William Marshall writing in 1796 describes the largest dairy farms as keeping between twenty and thirty beasts. Many smallholders kept a single cow; cottagers sometimes shared an animal if they could afford its upkeep.

What the dairymaid did have was a fine complexion, as the old saying 'as smooth as a milkmaid's skin' confirms. This was a result of working in close proximity to cattle and the consequent exposure to cowpox, a disease which carries no serious symptoms but which provides a partial immunity to smallpox, a virulent and often fatal disease that left its victims horribly scarred. Smallpox was ever-present in Britain and swept the countryside in sporadic outbreaks. The historian Thomas Macauley (1800–1859) described its effects:

> ...tormenting with constant fears all whom it had not yet stricken, leaving on those whose lives it spared the hideous traces of its power, turning the babe into a changeling at which the mother shuddered, and making the eyes and cheeks of the betrothed maiden objects of horror to the lover.

For women severe disfigurement meant not only loss of their beauty. From the medieval period until more enlightened times, the infliction of disease was considered a judgement by God on some personal wrongdoing – an embodiment of evil. Such attitudes were a long time in being dispelled among ill-educated elements of society.

Lady Mary Wortley Montague (1689–1762).

While smallpox showed no discrimination between rich and poor, there is some irony in the fact that one of its most celebrated victims should be a titled lady, whereas common milkmaids should escape its worst ravages.

Lady Mary Wortley Montague contracted smallpox in 1725 when in her mid twenties. It left her without eyelashes and with her skin permanently and deeply pitted. Two years after this, while living in Turkey, she noted that the local custom of children inhaling live smallpox virus from scabs taken from victims increased their chance of escaping the disease, a procedure known as variolation.

It was left to the scientist Edward Jenner to develop a control through vaccination that saw smallpox almost completely eradication in Western Europe. Noting the common observation that milkmaids were generally immune to smallpox, Jenner postulated that the pus in the blisters that milkmaids received from cowpox protected them from smallpox.

On 14 May 1796, Jenner tested his hypothesis by inoculating James Phipps, an eight-year-old boy who was the son of Jenner's gardener. He scraped pus from cowpox blisters on the hands of Sarah Nelmes, a milkmaid who had caught cowpox from a cow called Blossom. Jenner inoculated Phipps in both arms that day, subsequently producing in Phipps a fever and some uneasiness, but no full-blown infection. Later, he injected Phipps with variolous material, the routine method of immunization at that time. No disease followed. The boy was later challenged with variolous material and again showed no sign of infection. The cure had been found.

Edward Jenner (1749–1823).

*   *   *

An advertisement for a refrigerator from a catalogue of 1894 emphasises the point that it is 'constructed on a scientific basis' and science was certainly a buzz-word of the time. Such contraptions as this were for the well-off householder only. It comprised an insulated box cooled by a block of ice.

The preservation of food was a growing issue as the population moved further from the point of supply. Ice houses, built to keep a household supplied with ice year-round, were de rigueur in the grounds of larger houses, while supplying blocks of ice in towns and cities was a growing business, with Norway being the principal source of natural ice. Beginning in the mid 1850s, the trade reached its peak around 1900 at 400 000 tons per annum. Thereafter it simply 'melted away' and by 1915 the trade was entirely replaced by the manufacture of artificial ice and by refrigeration. However, the ice trade had been a vital factor in the early expansion of the dairying industry at the end of the Victorian era.

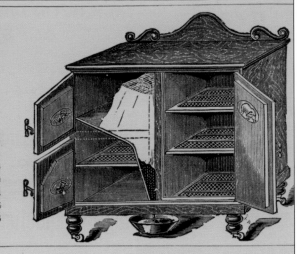

REFRIGERATORS.

ASH'S PATENT "SELF FEEDING" CABINET REFRIGERATOR OR ICE SAFE,

For use with Rough or Block Ice.

Is undoubtedly the **best** ever introduced, because unlike others it is constructed on a scientific basis, inasmuch that despite the gradual consumption of ice, the temperature remains practically the same throughout, thus the ice is economised and better results are obtained. This is fully explained with practical examples in the Company's Illustrated List (post free). N.B.—**Box Refrigerators** and all other kinds in Stock.

Just as domestic life at the end of the nineteenth century found new technology intruding upon age-old tradition, so aspects of farming began to welcome in new ideas and technology. Driven by the demands of a growing urban population, farmers looked to improve productivity and to explore new methods of safe and rapid supply. Nowhere was there a greater need for this than in dairying whose products, in the days before refrigeration, had a severely limited shelf life.

The work of the eighteenth century agricultural improvers, Jethro Tull, Lord Townshend, Arthur Young, Bakewell, Coke of Holkham among them, meant great advances in the breeding of cattle in order to improve milk yields. The consequence of increased food production overall led to a falling proportion of the workforce needed in farming throughout the nineteenth century leaving more to migrate to the industrial centres. These city dwellers in turn required more food and towards the end of the century the problem became one of supply.

On small farms and in remote parts of the country the farmer's wife continued to milk her cows and produce butter and cream, oblivious to the changes taking place elsewhere. Hand milking, usually twice a day, continued, the milk transferred from the cow into a galvanised steel pail that was carried to the dairy. Before hygiene became an issue it mattered little that grass or straw or other foreign bodies might fall into the pail while milking; these would be picked out or the milk strained through muslin into a milk can before being left to stand, sometimes placing the can in cool water. This would allow the cream to separate to be used in making clotted cream, butter and cheese. The separated milk would be for family use, in cooking, or for sale. Cool slate shelves in a windowless dairy were sufficient to keep milk fresh until it was consumed.

Above: Phillis Collet, the milkmaid carrying her milk pails at Foxworthy Farm on Dartmoor in 1907.

Top left: Bertha Groom, seventeen-year-old milkmaid at Mardleybury Farm, Hertfordshire c.1900.

Left: Mabel and Ada Friend milking at Wadland Barton, Northlew in Devon in 1918.

In 1885 in Cornwall a labourer's weekly pay was reported to be 16 shillings a week, but this included his daughter's wage as a milkmaid.

Jane Hicks, who was born in 1903, remembered her seventh birthday when she was told she would have something when she came home from school. The present turned out to be a wooden three-legged milking stool and a bucket!

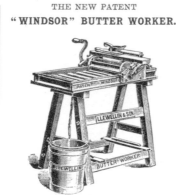

The Churn Question Settled ! The Best throughout the World !!

G. LLEWELLIN & SON

Are the Original Inventors and Manufacturers of

THE FAMOUS "ROYAL TRIANGULAR" CHURN.	THE NEW PATENT "WINDSOR" BUTTER WORKER.	AND THE "ROYAL ECCENTRIC" END-OVER CHURN.

Hand churning was notoriously onerous work and in certain weathers it took even longer for the milk to 'turn'. The resultant mix of raw butter and buttermilk was then strained and the solids were ready for 'working', either by hand on a wooden board or using a patent 'butter worker' as shown here.

Washing all the elements of the dairy on a Cornish farm. Cleanliness was essential for the churned milk would not 'turn' if it was contaminated. Note the wooden butter churn.

Opposite: Miss Collett, with Daisy, 1907.

Dairying, even on this scale, required quantities of clean water and on farms where this was in short supply, or had to be carried some distance, it meant additional work for the milkmaid, the farmer or his family, as a girl from Elmsett in Suffolk recalls:

We had a herd of cows so needed a lot of water when using the milking utensils, the churns and the ladles, and for dealing with the butter and cream. My brother Victor, sister Vera and I must have carried hundreds of gallons of water on our bicycles.

Traditional methods of making cream, churning butter and cheesemaking continued on smaller farms well into the twentieth century as a dairywoman working on a farm in Newdigate, Surrey, in the 1940s relates:

Miss Darbyshire owned a herd of pedigree Guernseys. Buckman the cowman lived in the cottage opposite. Betty Caspers was in charge of the dairy and there was another girl called Felicity. My first effort at hand-milking Floss was not very successful and we never milked the heavy milkers, Jan and Buttercup. At the end of the cowshed was a stall for the goat who ran with the herd.

The milk was weighed and poured into 10-gallon churns. In the dairy we filled half-pint, pint and quart bottles and fitted the cardboard disc caps ready for the milk rounds. The surplus was collected by the milk lorry. Another necessary job was washing bottles and sterilising all the milking buckets, strainers, etc. Miss Darbyshire and Betty drove a

A hand separator from around 1900 of the type that was used to separate the cream from milk, leaving skimmed milk which was often fed to calves. Note the version produced for use by women was half the size.

little green van to deliver the milk and Margaret and I harnessed Jimmy to the trap for deliveries to Cudworth.

It was an early start each morning to call the cows in from the field opposite. 'Come along, cow, cow...' Each knew her own stall and went straight to it to be chained up and washed before milking. After milking and mucking out we had a welcome breakfast seated round a long oak table.

Clotted or 'clouted' cream, a Westcountry speciality, was made from the full cream milk slowly heated or 'scalded' in a shallow pan which allowed the densest part of the cream content to rise to the top to form 'clots'.

Cheesemaking in Britain has a long and fascinating history with each region producing a distinctive variety based upon local tradition in the method of making, on the type of cattle, sheep or goats from which the milk was drawn, the process used in maturing and on the introduction of herbs and spice and other flavourings. Originally it was a way of preserving milk in a form that gave it a longer life and it became, particularly in Victorian Britain, a firm staple of the labourer's diet. The demand from cities was such that the production of cheese became centred in particular areas, notably in Cheshire and Leicestershire, and in Cheddar, Somerset. For a time Britain saw the demise of many local varieties, a situation reversed today by the flowering of many independent cheesemakers.

*　　*　　*

Making clotted cream in an old Devon open fireplace.

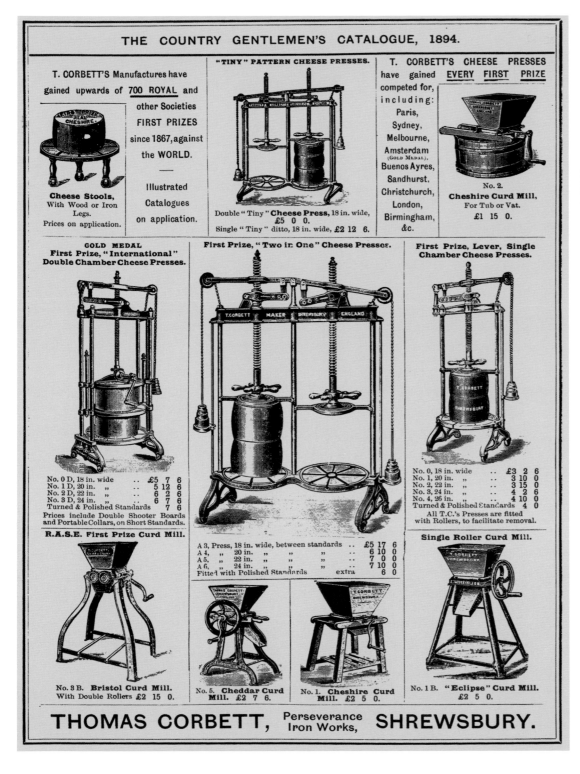

THE COUNTRY GENTLEMEN'S CATALOGUE, 1894.

T. CORBETT'S Manufactures have gained upwards of **700 ROYAL** and other Societies **FIRST PRIZES** since 1867, against the WORLD.

Illustrated Catalogues on application.

Cheese Stools, With Wood or Iron Legs. Prices on application.

"TINY" PATTERN CHEESE PRESSES.

Double "Tiny" **Cheese Press,** 18 in. wide, **£5 0 0.**
Single "Tiny" ditto, 18 in. wide, **£2 12 6.**

T. CORBETT'S CHEESE PRESSES have gained **EVERY FIRST PRIZE** competed for, including: Paris, Sydney, Melbourne, Amsterdam (GOLD MEDAL), Buenos Ayres, Sandhurst, Christchurch, London, Birmingham, &c.

No. 2. **Cheshire Curd Mill,** For Tub or Vat. **£1 15 0.**

GOLD MEDAL
First Prize, "International" Double Chamber Cheese Presses.

No. 0 D, 18 in. wide .. £5 7 6
No. 1 D, 20 in. „ .. 5 12 6
No. 2 D, 22 in. „ .. 6 2 6
No. 3 D, 24 in. „ .. 6 7 6
Turned & Polished Standards 7 6
Prices include Double Shooter Boards and Portable Collars, on Short Standards.

R.A.S.E. First Prize Curd Mill.

No. 3 B. **Bristol Curd Mill.** With Double Rollers £2 15 0.

First Prize, "Two in One" Cheese Presses.

A 3, Press, 18 in. wide, between standards .. £5 17 6
A 4, „ 20 in. „ „ „ .. 6 10 0
A 5, „ 22 in. „ „ „ .. 7 0 0
A 6, „ 24 in. „ „ „ .. 7 10 0
Fitted with Polished Standards extra 6 0

No. 5. **Cheddar Curd Mill. £2 7 6.**

No. 1. **Cheshire Curd Mill. £2 5 0.**

First Prize, Lever, Single Chamber Cheese Presses.

No. 0, 18 in. wide .. £3 2 6
No. 1, 20 in. „ .. 3 10 0
No. 2, 22 in. „ .. 3 15 0
No. 3, 24 in. „ .. 4 2 6
No. 4, 26 in. „ .. 4 10 0
Turned & Polished Standards 4 0
All T.C.'s Presses are fitted with Rollers, to facilitate removal.

Single Roller Curd Mill.

No. 1 B. **"Eclipse" Curd Mill. £2 5 0.**

THOMAS CORBETT, Perseverance Iron Works, **SHREWSBURY.**

A page from a catalogue of 1895 presenting a variety of cheesemaking machines including cheese mills and presses. Such machinery took some of the handwork out of dairying.

Condensed milk, milk from which the water has been removed, became a popular product from the early 1900s.

MILKMAID SWEETENED CONDENSED MILK — Best Full Cream Milk — PREPARED IN THE UNITED KINGDOM — PREPARADA EN EL REINO UNIDO — Regd. Trade Mark Marca Registrada — A NESTLÉ PRODUCT

From the end of the nineteenth century local dairies expanded and began supplying markets farther afield. Here workers are seen packing butter at Axe Vale Devon Dairy Supplies. Production on this scale required larger machinery as can be seen by the steam-driven churn on the right.

Enterprising farmers seized the opportunity to increase the size of their herds and to make the most of the faster transport links to the urban markets. Others expanded their dairying operation to supply local needs, delivering daily from the farm gate, while some opened dairy shops in villages that combined the provision of perishables along with general groceries.

Mrs Lister of the Chalk Farm dairy delivering milk near Lexham, Norfolk, in 1907.

THE DAIRYMAID

Every sort of vehicle was called into use from horse-drawn wagons to handcarts and bicycles. In some instances the milkmaid's duties were not confined to the dairy:

Phyllis started work by milking the shorthorns. She had just one Sunday off a month and another 'three parts of the day' when she could go home after milking the cows. Her day ran from 6am until 5pm but she was allowed home for breakfast with an hour off for lunch. She used a heavy bicycle with a milk carrier at the front to deliver quart bottles of milk to nearby properties. Phyllis earned a wage of £3 per week.

Milk delivery by horse and cart carried with it additional benefits for residents, as a villager in Hempnall, Norfolk, recalled:

Tom Dade delivered milk by pony and cart and gardeners would stand by with shovels in case they were lucky enough to find a deposit in the road.

Delivering milk door-to-door in Dawlish, Devon c.1900.

Hester Larke in the Hellesdon Dairy cart, Norfolk 1918.

Delivering milk in Helston, Cornwall, 1928.

Although not everyone was happy with such horticultural windfalls, as related by a resident of North Devon:

Reggie worked for Barnstaple Corporation cleaning the streets. Often, after he had cleaned one particular street on his route the milk cart came round and the horse left a deposit. The lady of the house outside which this misdemeanor usually happened complained to the Council and Reggie was made very aware of this by his superiors. The next time the horse 'performed' Reggie returned to the street, scooped the offending matter onto his Corporation shovel, knocked on the lady's door and, when she opened it, deposited the said matter in her hallway with a suitable comment!

Horses and carts, later motor vehicles, were also the means by which milk and other produce was taken to railway stations for onward transport by train to London and other cities. These were the famous milk trains that first ran to and from London in the 1830s, although at that time the capital still accommodated large herds of cows which provided the inhabitants daily with milk. In 1871 Express Dairies was one of the first operators to transport milk by rail on a large scale but other companies soon followed, many formed by farming co-operatives.

Churns were used to transport milk to the station, these being delivered by individual farmers or through a collection system that picked up the milk from churn stands built at convenient points on the roadside. Eventually the size of churns was standardised; first at 17 gallons and later at a more manageable 10 gallon size.

A late Victorian advertisement from Express Dairies.

Jim Copp, standing at the head of his horse, delivers milk from Middle Mill Farm to Uplyme in Dorset, 1930.

THE DAIRYMAID

By the early 1920 over 280 million gallons of milk were transported annually and later in the decade the railways introduced 3000 gallon rail tankers to replace churns, each tanker holding enough milk to supply 35 000 people, although much of the transported milk was destined for the growing numbers of factories who required milk for their products. This included cheese and butter factories, dried milk and chocolate manufacturers, and pig breeding units which used the whey by-product as feed.

But easier rail access was by no means without its problems for small-scale farmers who in the 1890s now tried to sell their dairy products in the local market against quality produce brought in by rail. In Cornwall for instance, following tradition, a number of farmers stored their milk and butter until they accumulated enough to take it to market and, as a result, their butter acquired a 'greyish-tinge', while their milk was described as being 'tinctured with a variety of flavours'.

Above: A Cornish farmer's wife handling 17 gallon milk churns c.1930.

Below: Churns await collection at Walling-ford Station in Oxfordshire, 1937.

THE FARMER'S WIFE

According to authors Schwartz and Parker in *The Book of Lanner* the competition from 'foreign' imports into Cornwall in the 1890s caused great consternation:

To their horror, local farmers found that the Cornish housewife would pay a premium for Danish and Dutch butter, bacon, eggs and cheese, standardised and graded for quality, size and colour. To save the Cornish farmer from disaster, food processing factories were needed, and Cornwall's modernising bourgeoisie of industrialists, merchants and bankers rallied round to finance them.

Erecting the factories was one thing, getting farmers to deliver a standard output of uniform quality at regular times was quite another. Although farmers were realistic and practical, they were temperamentally opposed to becoming – as they saw it – slaves to a factory system. The result was some spectacular failures. One dairy-processing factory at Truro closed because farmers, in open carts in warm weather, delivered cream that went sour before it arrived. Another, in Helston, collapsed partly because the quality of milk was poor, partly because in times of drought, farmers switched to supplying the growing tourist industry.

Women dairy workers at the Nestlé factory in Staverton, Wiltshire in 1905. The former cloth factory had been purchased by the Anglo-Swiss Condensed Milk Company in the 1890s and began producing canned milk under the Ideal Milk brand. By 1919 the factory employed over 300 workers at which time the factory was using the milk from over 6500 cows a day.

Tainted milk, rancid butter and stale cream was not unusual in the days before refrigeration and sell-by dates, but the bulk supply of untreated milk from a multitude of sources posed a serious health risk. This was exacerbated by a largely unregulated trade in foodstuffs, both in town and country, and the growth in small shops and tea rooms selling dairy produce. There are few better mediums for growing microbes than warm milk and lengthy journey times between farm and customer increased the chances of disease through drinking raw milk. In England and Wales between 1912 and 1937 some 65 000 people died from tuberculosis contracted from consuming such milk.

Chemists had for centuries understood the process, known as pasteurisation and named after Louis Pasteur the nineteenth century scientist, by which the quality of wine could be preserved by heating it. Towards the end of the 1800s milk was heat treated in this way and while not killing all bacteria the process significantly reduced the risk of falling ill through milk consumption.

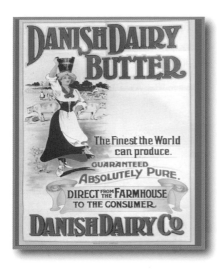

Competition from abroad, particularly the dairying countries of western Europe who used advertising to its best effect, threatened the livelihood of British farmers.

Milk delivery to an early nineteenth century refreshment room providing teas, pastries and sandwiches to tourists to Sheringham, Norfolk. A small sign advertises 'nursery milk' for sale.

79

As dairy farms grew larger so more workers were required and estate farms would have their own regimes to ensure hygiene. This photo, taken in 1900, shows the milking team at Barton Farm near Cerne Abbas in Dorset. Mr Seward the farm bailiff sits in the centre row. Note the traditional smocks and bonnets worn by the dairymaids.

In the late 1890s the government and local authorities recognised an urgent need to reduce the risks of food contamination in dairy products and to encourage good practice among those engaged in dairying. Education was seen as a way to improve the quality of locally produced butter and cheese and so the recently formed County Councils, with money available from the Technical Instruction Grants, financed travelling dairy schools to tour the rural district and town dairies.

THE DAIRYMAID

Each region had its own policy regarding how these schools were run. In Leicestershire, Nottinghamshire and Derbyshire the authorities combined to create a college based at a farm of 160 acres near Kingston-on-Soar. The Midland Dairy Institute as it was known was opened in September 1895.

In other areas of the country teaching sessions would be held at selected farms, in village halls and in schoolrooms, the courses varying in length from a few days to a week or more. Certificates were issued to those who had successfully completed the course and while boys and young men attended, the vast majority of students were girls and young women. Such schools continued well into the 1940s, with the need for training being stepped up during both world wars.

Staff and students at Cornwall County Council's Dairy School in Stithians, 1914. The boys in the front row display a board of cheeses while the girl, centre, hold a sheet containing the rules of the school. Photographs of similar schools from up and down the country show a similar proportion of female to male participants.

Above: A certificate presented to Millie Lutry in 1916 confirming her proficiency in milking.

Right: Women students at Somerset County Council's buttermaking class, 1927.

Some caution should be exercised concerning the number of women engaged in dairying, and indeed in many parts of agriculture in which they have played a significant role. The facts are that even in dairying, where they figure large, throughout most of history more men were employed than women. It is simply that proportional to the total female workforce a higher percentage of women were employed in dairying than in most other areas of farming. Such statistics generally apply throughout this book up to the period after the First World War when the number of women as a proportion of the national workforce began to close the gap on men.

Slowly but surely the changes that came in with the new century eroded old traditions and by the mid 1950s the role of the milkmaid had all but disappeared. The fresh-faced maid carrying her milk pail out to the cows in the meadow, an image so beloved of Victorian artists, was possibly now labouring in a milk factory, dressed in a starched uniform working alongside hundreds of others.

On the farm, the invention of an efficient vacuum operated milking machine in 1907 (one that imitated the action of the suckling calf) and the introduction of automated processes for separation, bottling etc. reduced the need for dairymen and women. By the 1930s only the smallest dairy farms, those with only a milch cow or two, resisted the opportunity to install milking machines, second-hand models being plentiful and affordable. The industrialisation of dairying was complete.

Feeding the Family

Pray Sir Billy, do not weep,
We've stolen one of your fat sheep.
For you are rich, and we are poor,
And when that's had, we'll come for more.

Note pinned on a Cornish farmer's gate c.1850

In an earlier chapter the layout of the farm kitchen was looked at in the context of the fireplace around which the domestic life of the farm revolved. The introduction of the cast-iron range towards the end of the nineteenth century transformed the life of the farmer's wife and heralded in new methods of preparing and cooking food. Before then cooking was done on an open fire using pots and crude utensils all of which limited even the most adventurous housewife regarding recipes.

'Old Woman Peeling Potatoes' by Walter Langley (1852-1922).

The heart of the home. A Lakeland kitchen photographed around 1900. The kitchen range here is an early type that still has an open grate over which hangs a kettle for hot water. On the right is a small oven with a hinged door – an updated equivalent of the brick or clay bread oven found in medieval hearths. Bunches of herbs and dried hams hang from the beams.

83

A medieval boar hunt. Hunting and eating wild game was then the exclusive preserve of the aristocracy, with severe punishments meted out to those who transgressed. The Anglo Saxon Chronicle relates the law laid down by William the Conqueror who:

"....set many deer free, and laid a law upon it, that whoever slew hart or hind should be blinded. As he forbade the killing of harts he forbade the killing of boars, and he loved the stags as if he were their father. He decreed also that hares must go free. The rich complained, the poor lamented; but he was so hard he set their hate at naught..."

The medieval poor were confined to three meals a day, with breakfast taken at sunrise comprising bread taken with ale. A midday meal was taken out into the fields and might include bread with cheese or meat if available, also washed down with ale. A final meal of vegetable pottage warmed over the fire served for the last meal of the day, again with bread and ale. Fish and meat varied this frugal diet if and when they came to hand. Milk was drunk, but with water often too contaminated the main drink was a crude beer, brewed by most cottagers for home consumption only.

White bread made from wheat flour was preferred but was denied to the peasantry who could only afford the dark, heavy bread made from rye and barley. In times of poor harvests, when grain was in short supply, peas, beans and acorns would be used to make bread. Milling grain was outlawed except in the Lord of the Manor's grist mills; baking bread too could only be done in the Lord's ovens.

Pottage, a kind of thick soup made from oats, perhaps with added vegetables, was a staple of the medieval diet. Pork and mutton was eaten when available – with every part of the animal, including its blood, being made good use of. Wild game, fish and fowl was the property of the Lord and the poor were forbidden to catch them, though vermin such as squirrels and hedgehogs were freely hunted for food.

Such poor diet resulted in short lives among the medieval peasantry, with high mortality rates in children. Adult life expectancy in 1500 was 35 years with two-thirds of all children dying before the age of four, compared to the aristocracy where a full three-score years and ten was their allotted span. Aristocratic estates provided the wealthy with freshly killed meat and river fish, as well as fresh fruit and vegetables. Cooked dishes were heavily flavoured with valuable spices such as caraway, nutmeg, cardamom, ginger and pepper. Other commonly used ingredients included cane sugar, almonds, and dried fruits such as dates, figs or raisins.

A significant number of recipe manuscripts survive from the medieval period but it is from the Tudors that the template for all future cookery books spring. These offered recipes and menu suggestions along with tips for the housewife covering issues such as childcare and health. Among these is a *Propre Newe Booke of Cookerye* written for ladies running their own households and published in 1545. In the following century Gervase Markham's *The English Huswife, Containing the Inward and Outward Virtues Which Ought to Be in a Complete Woman* was first published in 1615. There followed many others: Hannah Woolley's *The Queen-like Closet* (1672), Richard Bradley's *The Country Housewife* (1732), *The Art of Cookery Made Plain and Easy* by Hannah Glasse (1747) and the doyen of them all, Mrs Beeton's *Book of Household Management* published in 1861.

Of course all these were only of use to those who could read – a relatively small number confined almost entirely to the upper classes in the sixteenth and seventeenth centuries. They serviced the needs of those running households with servants, those feeding large extended families, and households providing feasts for the entertainment of guests. Even the popularity of Mrs Beeton was confined to the aspirant Victorian middle classes; she had little to offer the rural poor. Their needs were met by more practical books and pamphlets, often with a religious undertone, that concentrated less on 'first catch your hare' and more on 'first boil your cabbage'. One of the most enduring of these, published in 1856, seeing its final edition in 1976 having sold 1.5 million copies, was *Enquire Within*. Essentially an encyclopedia of useful tips, it contained in its introduction the following:

"Whether You Wish to Model a Flower in Wax;
to Study the Rules of Etiquette;
to Serve a Relish for Breakfast or Supper;
to Plan a Dinner for a Large Party or a Small One;
to Cure a Headache;
to Make a Will;
to Get Married;
to Bury a Relative;
Whatever You May Wish to Do, Make, or to Enjoy,
Provided Your Desire has Relation to the Necessities of Domestic Life,
I Hope You will not Fail to 'Enquire Within.'" – Editor.

Above: Puddings & pastries from Mrs Beeton.

Below: The village street in Ilsington, Devon, c.1900 showing the traditional arrangement for the community's water supply. On the left of the street one can see water running from a granite spout. This is the potwater leat from which 'clean' water was taken. On the right is the gutter for disposing of dirty water, the slopwater leat.

The daily round of the rural housewife's domestic duties centred on the supply of water. While beer and cider were the thirst-quenchers of choice, water was the first essential in cooking.

From earliest time farms and other dwellings were sited as close as possible to a reliable source of water. Streams and rivers were the obvious choice but not where the danger of flooding was apparent. In dry areas, on chalk lands for instance, settlements grew along the spring line at the foot of scarp slopes. Farmers and villagers dug ponds that would fill naturally from springs and from rainfall and these provided a store of water when other sources ran dry. Dew ponds were built on higher ground for watering stock. In upland areas particularly, farmers took the lead from millers and created artificial water courses that carried a supply from a known clean and reliable source to the farmhouse. These leats could sometimes run over several miles, serving a number of farms and villages along the way.

Where surface water was not available a well would have to be dug until a potable supply was reached, not always a foregone conclusion as reported from Newtown on the Isle of Wight:

On 19 October 1893 the Parochial Committee met and resolved to obtain a water-supply for Newtown. Initially, the committee blanched at the proposed cost, and suggested that,

Above: Drawing water at the village pump, Dartington in Devon in 1890.

Right: Water sources also provided food. In this evocative photograph taken c.1900 near Ivybridge in Devon, a woman gathers water-cress from a local stream.

instead, the parish should supply each household with a tank or reservoir for rainwater, but eventually agreed to seek a loan in order to sink a well 30 feet deep. A tender of £66 was accepted for completing the well and fitting a pump. Initially, the plan was to dig a 60-foot well, but at half that depth water analysis revealed mineral contamination. The well was rarely used, the water being a little brackish and there being so many private wells and springs in the village anyway.

In former times water would be drawn from the well by a rope or chain pulley with a bucket attached, this arrangement was later replaced by a pump that saved much labour but still required priming, while wintry weather posed other problems:

A group of children in Helston, Cornwall, washing vegetables in the river.

Above: The common nettle illustrated in a nineteenth century herbal. Nettle leaves were used in teas and salads and the fibres employed in the making of cloth.

Below: Husband and wife freshwater fishing on Ranworth Broad, Norfolk c.1900.

We had to get the water from the well in the field next to the house and later from a pump at the back of the house – this pump would freeze in winter and then straw was burnt around it so that it could be defrosted.

And other surprises were in store as a resident of Chittlehamholt in Devon recalled:

There was a water pump just inside the lane which needed to be primed before you used it as all sorts would come out, including frogs. This water was collected by us in pitchers and supplied all our needs at the cottage.

Watercourses also provided food and it was part of the country wife's armoury to possess a wide knowledge of edible plants and herbs, especially medicinal plants, known as 'physics' In the days before it was farmed watercress had for centuries been gathered from streams and eaten raw or boiled. Ramsons (with their garlic smell), also called water leeks, were used to make a fish sauce, and Marsh Mallow was gathered by herbalists to use as poultices and for cough cures.

Rivers and streams also produced fish although, as with game, the medieval poor were forbidden in law to catch fish without the landowner's permission. Freshwater fish such as carp were bred in ponds from the medieval period onwards and native species were plentiful in pre-industrialised British rivers including pike and perch. A recipe from *The Country Housewife and Lady's Director*:

Perch are now very good, the large ones for stewing, as recommended for carp, or boiled or fryd, or else in the Dutch manner which is to boil the perches with salt in the water, and parsley roots and parsley leaves, to be brought to the table in the water they are boiled in, and eaten with bread and butter.

In the Christian religion Fridays were fast days; meat, and animal products such as milk, cheese, butter and eggs, were not allowed, only fish. Fasting was observed on other days too, including Lent and Advent. This meant a widespread trade in fish, mainly sea fish, caught and brought inland to be sold at markets, the majority dried, salted or smoked.

In Victorian Britain salmon and oysters were so common that they became dietary staples of the poor, as Charles Dickens portrays in *The Pickwick Papers*:

"Not a very nice neighbourhood this, sir," said Sam, with a touch of the hat, which always preceded his entering into conversation with his master.
"It is not indeed, Sam," replied Mr Pickwick, surveying the crowded and filthy street through which they were passing.

"It's a very remarkable circumstance, sir," said Sam, "that poverty and oysters always seems to go together."

"I don't understand, Sam," said Mr. Pickwick.

"What I mean, sir," said Sam, "is, that the poorer a place is, the greater call there seems to be for oysters. Look here, sir; here's a oyster stall to every half dozen houses. The streets lined vith 'em. Blessed if I don't think that ven a man's wery poor, he rushes out of his lodgings and eats oysters in reg'lar desperation."

As with perishable dairy produce, the availability of fish increased with the arrival of the railways, and fish trains ran to and from the major fishing ports just as milk trains journeyed daily from the agricultural regions of the country. This and, later, the availability of ice and refrigeration, brought fish regularly into the hands of the rural housewife even in the heart of the country, although Friday remained *the* day for eating fish well into the twentieth century. For the poorest family there was always something a little less expensive:

Cods' Heads: In some places, fishmongers take the heads off their codfish before they cut up the rest of the fish to retail it; the heads are sold cheap; and when they can be had for somewhere about twopence each, they are well worth buying. They are in season through the whole of autumn and winter; and we have enjoyed many a cheap fish-treat with a dish of cods' heads, which contain several of the tit-bits prized by epicures,

A very early image of a Newlyn fish seller, or 'jowster' c.1870 from the collection of Cornish photographer Reg Watkiss. These fishwives would buy fish on the beach as the catches were landed and walk to inland towns and villages selling their wares.

Mrs Nellie Grimmer sold fish from her cart as she travelled from village to village in Norfolk. Here she is photographed c.1920 in Happisburgh.

Women cocklers at Dawlish, Devon c.1910.

namely, the tongue, the cheek-pieces, and the nape of the neck. The only inconvenience attending cods' heads is, that if there are several, they require a large kettle to boil them in; but they can be cooked one or two at a time, reserving the flesh from the second batch for next day's use. After taking out the eyes, wash the heads, drain them, and if you can let them lie all night with a little salt sprinkled over them. Put them into a kettle of boiling water, and boil from a quarter of an hour to twenty minutes, according to size. Dish them on a strainer, if you can, and help with a spoon. For sauce, oiled butter is good.

*   *   *

The kitchen garden or an allotment was a vital part of the farm. While by no means the sole province of the housewife, it provided a ready and vital source of vegetables and culinary herbs. It was usual for the strip of land chosen for the garden to be close to the farmhouse or cottage, sheltered ground, making the preparation of the soil, sowing and gathering of the crop more convenient. It also meant that predators could be more easily controlled; rabbits and various birds being a constant menace.

In early times such gardens were vital in feeding the family but as the centuries passed, the garden, while still providing a ready source of cheap and nutritious food, became more of pastime, indulging the pleasure of gardening. Fierce competition blazed at the annual flower and veg show to who could produce the finest.

Though a decidedly romantic interpretation, 'The Flower Pickers' by Ernest Walbourn (1872-1927) contains all the elements of the cottage garden. In the shelter of the old thatched dwelling, alongside the well, flowers bloom, while on the other side of the path a plot is given over to cabbages and other vegetables.

'Zander' Crout hoeing weeds in his Dartmoor cottage garden watched by his wife in the 1920s. By this time, though providing valued additions to the family diet, gardening for pleasure was becoming the British passion. It was only at the outbreak of the Second World War that the country once more turned to growing vegetables in earnest.

Historian P.H. Ditchfield author of *The Cottages and Village Life of Rural England* sums up the practical and the pleasurable side of gardening in 1912:

> *The garden has often a little orchard attached to it, or fruit trees growing amongst the cabbages and potatoes... Pear blossom, cherry blossom, make the garden gay and bright, and we trust that no cold winds or late frosts may come to blight the prospect of a good fruit harvest. 'God tempers the wind to the shorn lamb' and often in the sheltered garden of a cottage the fruit sets and grows and ripens far better than in the more exposed rectory pleasance, and brings grist to the labourer's scanty store... Such country customs and the possession of a good garden which will produce vegetables for the whole year for the rustic family, and provide interest and employment in the evenings, and a perpetual delight to the agricultural labourer, make country life far better than the lot of those who have to live in towns.*

Factories could now bottle and can fruit and other produce that made it long-lasting, cheap and easily transported.

By the early years of the twentieth century faster transport brought food to the doorsteps of all but the most remote village. Canned and processed food, heavily advertised and promoted, offered a more exciting prospect than home-grown produce. The knowledge that formerly allowed the countrywomen to identify hundreds of edible wild plants lost its value, diluted by modernity; a wisdom destined to be confined to folklore.

THE FARMER'S WIFE

Enterprising gardeners could now sell excess produce through the village shop, many of which opened in the downstair rooms of cottages, others incorporating themselves into Post Offices. A village square in the early 1900s:

Mary Charity Gooding of High Bickington in Devon c.1900. Mary owned the village stores which she ran with her husband. Bottles, jars, cans and boxes of food line the shelves. Villagers could now get their hands on a multitude of provisions, easing the pressure on the housewife to provide for the family from her own resources.

Lydia French had a shop opposite the church. The little town or overgrown village had no market, but there were fairs held in the space before the church on one side and Lydia French's shop on the other twice in the year. Both were cattle fairs, frequented by farmers. On such occasions bullocks ran about with tails lifted, yelling men and barking dogs behind and before them, and made either for the churchyard wall or for Lydia French's shop window. On these occasions Lydia French's shop was full of customers. She, moreover, had a good clientele in the entire parish, but experienced less difficulty in disposing of her goods than in getting her bills paid.

FEEDING THE FAMILY

Demand from the growing populace encouraged more farmers to move away from traditional crops and into the more lucrative area of market gardening. Once again the railways provided the means of transporting produce rapidly to where the demand, and therefore the price it could be sold for, was greatest. Highly labour-intensive, particularly when it came to harvesting the crop, the gardening skills of the rural workforce came into their own. Cash crops such as soft fruit and flowers joined the long-established harvests of orchard fruit and hops for which tasks gangs of hired labour would travel the country. A Cornish woman recalls the pleasure and pains of working in the strawberry fields:

Strawberries had to be hoed; we quite liked this because a gang of us could gossip, going up and down the rows. Most of us wore shorts, and I remember one girl trying to hoe with one leg turned to the sun to brown her legs equally. Then came the strawberry picking; if it was a good crop and it always seemed to be, we worked all day in the blazing sun, and back in the evening after getting the evening meal for our families. The proper way to pick strawberries was astride the beds, so both sides were properly picked. By the end of the evening, we knelt, we sat, we sweated. I can assure you that the pleasure of filling your mouth while you picked soon wore off! There was a lot of strawberry jam in the pantries of the village in those days. It was of course seasonal work, and it seemed to be always raining when planting or cutting cabbage.

A gang of strawberry pickers in the fields near Strumpshaw, Norfolk around 1910.

Apple pickers in the orchards near Cullompton, Devon, c.1900. Apple trees were growing in the UK well before the Romans came but it was they who introduced organised cultivation. The apple is thought to be the only fruit cultivated by the medieval farmer although pears, quinces etc. were available from the wild. The Normans brought their own methods of cider making with them and introduced new varieties. 'Vargis' (or verjuice) was a concoction made from fermented crab apples and was used to cure sprains and rheumatic ailments.

Women and children among the raspberry canes in Norfolk c.1920.

Wild fruit and berries gathered to supplement the family diet continued to be picked though the need to do so was reduced due to the availability of shop-bought produce. However apple orchards, producing fruit for cider-making or for eating, expanded and required a considerable workforce at picking time. Children worked alongside their mothers, some as young as five or six years of age. Teachers in their daily log books constantly complained of absenteeism among their pupils, although in some regions the school year was arranged to accommodate harvesting, as at Carhampton in North Devon in the last years of the nineteenth century:

Children did not attend school when they were needed on the farm: for example birdkeeping, haymaking, wort picking, harvest, gleaning, blackberrying, mushrooming and picking potatoes. The parents' employers expected these chores and the resulting income was essential for family budgets so summer holidays were determined by the agricultural year. School managers decided the length of holidays according to whortleberry picking and harvesting: if the fruit was ripe early the children were absent.

FEEDING THE FAMILY

In hop growing areas the influx of itinerant workers who followed the harvest caused consternation among the locals. In Worcestershire between the wars several thousand temporary workers arrived to bring in the hop harvest, with farmers providing barrack-like blocks to house them. A resident of Bransford in the county recalls these times when she was a young girl:

In September, the hop picking would be in full swing and nearly all the women and girls in the village would be involved. My sister and I longed to go, but mother always said there were lots of tinkers and gypsies there and she wouldn't be there to look after us, so we were not allowed to. However, we often sneaked into the hop yard and joined our friends, though we were in trouble when we got home and mother could smell the scent of the hops on us and see our blackened fingers. We were fascinated by the hop-pickers' barracks where the Black Country pickers stayed, and the lovely blazing fires where they cooked their food, whilst their lingo was like a foreign language to us.

In September and October thousands of workers travelled from farm to farm hop picking, bringing tents and caravans or living in barracks provided by the farmers. These shacks were notoriously primitive and eventually required government inspectors to ensure their habitability. The author George Orwell records the words of hop pickers in Kent in the late 1920s: 'A holiday with pay.' 'Keep yourself all the time you're down there, pay your fare both ways and come back five quid in pocket.'

*   *   *

An English hand-coloured postcard dated 1913 of a farmer's wife, a cockerel and hen.

The care of what was generally know as 'the fowl' also appears to have traditionally fallen to the farmer's wife. In this regard ducks, chickens and geese were the principal domesticated farmyard birds, although others such a doves (pigeons), guinea fowl and peacocks were also kept. Wild birds were also caught and eaten including wood-pigeon, rooks, cranes, herons and swans. In medieval times, excepting those wild animals which it was illegal for the poor to catch, few wild birds or their eggs were off the menu, including songbirds such as larks and linnets.

The regional variations in what types of domestic bird were most popular in these earliest times are difficult to ascertain but figures from a study of estates in Norfolk between 1240 and 1400AD suggest that of chickens, geese and ducks, chickens comprised around 55 per cent of such fowls kept, geese 40 percent and ducks about 5 per cent. Turkeys were introduced into Europe from the Americas by returning Spanish explorers and did not become common until the seventeenth century.

By the nineteenth century selective breeding led to a wide range of recognised breeds of chickens, some prolific egg layers, others prized for their meat. Defined breeds of geese and ducks also were now commonly appearing in the farmyard.

Those attentive to their brood of hens had to be constantly vigilant:

Much of her spare time was devoted to her chickens, which fully repaid her for the care given them. She was not particular about fancy stock, but had quite a variety – White

Most country dwellers would keep a few hens and here the chickens are encouraged to appear in the photograph by Mr Leaman who feeds them from a small bowl. The family gather outside their cottage in Devon in 1915.

The daily feeding ritual as a flurry of poultry gather around Mrs Flood at Waterloo Farm in Norfolk c.1900

Leghorns, Brown Leghorns, big, fat, motherly old Brahma hens that had raised a brood of as many as thirty-five little chicks at one time, a few snow-white, large Plymouth Rocks and some gray Barred ones.

Free ranging fowl would be prey to all kinds of wildlife, in particular foxes, and securing the wandering birds in their house at night could be problematic, especially if the hen had built a nest and laid eggs in some obscure hedge bottom. Maintaining a flock of birds meant keeping a rooster in order to ensure clutches of eggs were fertile; vital before the days of buying-in day-old chicks.

In order to keep layers healthy, a sizeable flock would require food additional to what the hens could forage for themselves. Many a farmhouse kitchen was pervaded with the sour smell of a pot of mash simmering away on the stove top. The appearance of the farmer's wife with a bucketful of feed or household scraps would be the signal for the hens to converge upon her, fighting over every morsel and chasing each other around the yard. A Somerset shopkeeper recalls the 1920s:

Nearly all the cottagers kept poultry in their back gardens. We kept large wooden vats containing wheat, maize and layers mash. These were sold in large brown paper bags holding either 7 or 3½lbs. We also sold Karswood Poultry Spice in small packets. This was added to the wet mash and vegetable mixture in order to encourage laying. Chickens were hatched under broody hens and a china egg was kept in the nest boxes to encourage hens to use them. Empty orange crates were in great demand for this purpose.

Plucking ducks outside the aptly named Plume of Feathers Inn, Princetown on Dartmoor in the 1930s.

THE FARMER'S WIFE

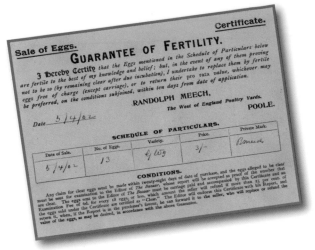

The sale of surplus eggs, pullets and plucked and drawn chickens in the local market provided additional pin money for the housewife. Others looked to chicken farming as a more substantial source of income, which in turn provided local employment, as a resident of Lanner in Cornwall in the 1930s recalls:

> *Many local farms raised poultry before the war, and Mary Job was frequently asked to kill, pluck, draw and dress poultry, a job she did at home to earn extra money, charging three pence for a chicken, sixpence for a duck and a shilling for a goose. She hung the birds upside down by their legs from the trees in her orchard and then slit their throats. After they had been left to bleed, she brought them in to be plucked and drawn. During the busy season at Christmas and Easter, the floor would be covered with a thick layer of feathers each day.*

Greater mobility meant that the farmer's wife no longer need to 'set' her own eggs but could have fertile eggs delivered from a dealer. In 1902 thirteen 'guaranteed' eggs cost about 3 pennies each.

Perhaps a more realistic image of keeping poultry. This is the muddy yard at Crockwell Farm, Kingsteignton in Devon in 1900 with the farmer's wife Mrs Stentiford surrounded by ducks, chickens and turkeys.

For the poor cottager, chicken would only be on the menu if a bird stopped laying or seemed sickly. In past centuries the birds were much smaller than those we know of today. Elizabeth Moxon in her book *English Housewifry*, published in 1764, provides a recipe for 'a proper side-dish' beginning: 'Take four or five small chickens...'.

Eating fresh meat was the privilege for those higher up the social scale in medieval times, the diet of the poor being restricted to a cereal-based pottage, 'frumenty', or 'mortrew' which contained some meat. Pigs were kept by the peasantry who held rights to graze them in the forests and their meat would be preserved, pickled, salted or smoked. In times of great need the poor would forage for what food they could, the more palatable meat coming from squirrels and other small vermin; larger game including deer, hares and wild boar being the exclusive quarry of the nobility.

Rabbit meat was much favoured and because they breed profusely it was readily available. Artificial warrens were built to maintain a ready supply, enclosed to discourage the rabbits from escaping and to deter predators, with the warrener and his family often living nearby, harvesting the animals as required. Rabbits were one of the few wild animals to be husbanded in this way.

In later centuries individual farmers owned the rights over the rabbits on their land and, while warrens survived in some areas into the twentieth century, the favoured method of hunting them was with ferrets, sometimes using dogs to drive rabbits into nets spread across a field. Shooting parties would make a sport of rabbiting, with large catches providing meat and rabbit skins for the fur trade.

A fourteenth century manuscript illustration of women hunting rabbits with a ferret. Ferrets are still used today though most hunting of rabbits is for their control rather than for food. Gin traps, now illegal, were also used as these ensured the animal and its skin was undamaged. The need for control even today has some validity as eight rabbits consume as much as one sheep.

A Boxing Day rabbit shoot at Hindringham, Norfolk in the early 1900s. On a farm in the Westcountry one boy recalls: 'Boxing Day consisted of shooting pigeons and rabbits and I can remember being very tired carrying them home.'

Writing in his Cottage Economy *in 1833, William Cobbett eschews hunting and suggests husbandry as a better alternative:*

Rabbits are really profitable. Three does and a buck will give you a rabbit to eat for every three days in the year, which is a much larger quantity of food than any man will get by spending half his time in the pursuit of wild animals, to say nothing of the toil, the tearing of clothes, and the danger of pursuing the latter.

For the housewife a rabbit provided a versatile choice of meal, from stews to rabbit pie or a fricasee. An Elizabethan recipe offered yet another alternative:

To boil a Rabbet with Claret Wine
Boil a Rabbet as before, then slice Onions and a Carrot root, a few Currans and a Fagot
of sweet herbs, and a little Salt, minced Parsley, Barberries picked, large Mace, Nutmeg
and Ginger, put all these into a Pipkin with the Rabbet, half a Pound of Butter, and a
Pint of Claret Wine, let them boil together till it be enough, then serve it upon Sippets.

Stories abound of the time during harvest when the approach of the reapers with their scythes drove rabbits from the corn, or when the mechanical binders gradually circling the crop left a small patch remaining in which the rabbits were hiding:

Many of the children in Cullompton would spend the time rabbiting in cornfields. Every-
one had a stick with a knob on the end, with which to kill the rabbits as we chased
them out of the corn. If the farmer in whose field you were gave you a rabbit to take
home, that was a couple of days' dinner. In fact, in the summer time we lived on rabbit
stew, rabbit pie and roast rabbit.

Shotguns at the ready, farmers in Sculthorpe, Norfolk, are ready for rabbits making a dash from the standing corn as the reaper closes in. A photograph from around 1910.

Rabbits were an important part of a farmer's income, considered a crop like any other. But when rabbits were plentiful, everyone benefited, as a correspondent to the *Royal Cornwall Gazette* wrote in 1906:

When the long day's work is over and the harvesters tramp home to the village, there is not a man or boy amongst them who has not a bundle of dead rabbits to carry. When one considers how little of butcher's meat can ever find its way into a cottage when the average-earner's income is 13–15 shillings a week, one can understand the value of these rabbits at harvest-time.

* * *

Meat from sheep was the most commonly eaten as mutton, an animal at least two years of age, but even this was considered something of a luxury. In the Middle Ages sheep were valued as much for their wool, for their skins (for parchment) and for butter and milk, as for their meat.

'The roast beef of Old England' has been long heralded as the nation's signature dish. Much of this has to do with Shakespeare whose Henry V has the French lords quailing at the thought of British soldiers fighting like devils after 'great meals of beef'. Fictional characters John Bull and Mr Pickwick perpetuate the myth. Certainly the wealthy have always enjoyed the best cuts – a baron of beef being the most legendary of these.

The farmer's wife was much more likely to have busied herself with what remained after the best cuts had been sold. From the tongue to the tail and everything between, the housewife had a culinary use for it, even to the bones and the blood. Regional

Vernon Hunt bringing home a rabbit for the pot at Foxworthy Farm c.1925.

The Shambles in Dunster, Somerset, a photograph dated 1865. The building dates from 1825. Shambles is the name given to an open air slaughterhouse or meat market where the housewife would come to buy meat in medieval times. Little by way of hygiene was carried out here with blood and offal washed into open gullies, noisome and often the cause of complaint. In 1853 for instance, at Lanner in Cornwall, butchers were ordered 'that all offal and everything offensive that comes from their slaughterhouses were moved to such safe distance from every dwelling house as shall meet the approval of the inspectors'.

variations on the use of offal survive today as black pudding, haggis and faggots – all these familiar to the farmhouse cook of the past. What couldn't be eaten immediately was salted, pickled, dried or smoked so that it might provide for the family later. Only when the village butcher's shop came within reach of most did this kind of food preparation in the home begin to fall away.

Charles Dickens is said to have inspired modern Christmas celebrations and the traditional image of a butcher's shop front hung with turkeys and sides of beef persists even today. Recalling her Devon childhood in the early 1900s Irene Sampson of North Tawton relates:

We were self-sufficient for most food. We took animals for slaughter to two butchers in Exbourne – Glanville's and Chapple's. We bought in large quarters of beef, which didn't last long with all of us. On Christmas Eve we entertained the workmen and their families at an evening meal of roast sirloin of beef and suet pudding.

As the communal shambles-type of market-place were closed, butchers moved into their own shops. By late Victorian times almost every town, and many villages, supported their own butcher who would also act as slaughterer for the local farmers. Here Mr and Mrs Massey and staff display their wares outside the shop in North Newton, Somerset, c.1920.

While it is no longer acceptable to view women in the kind of domesticity summed up in the German expression *Kinder, Küche, Kirche*, the British housewife's role in the home was reinforced from generation to generation through family, religion and, from the nineteenth century, through school. It was not until the 1960s that boys were invited to participate in what were then called domestic science lessons. As late as 1926, as young girl, Kathy Pointer from Swaffham, Norfolk, recalls going from school to the local workhouse in order to be taught lessons in laundry and cooking.

Girls of Cornwood School in Devon posing for their cookery class photograph in 1911.

* * *

Keeping a pig was universal for country people from Norman times through to the early twentieth century. It was one of the few concessions granted to medieval peasantry by their overlords, that of the right of pannage – that is permission to graze domestic pigs on common land and in woodland. Here acorns and beech mast formed a large part of their diet as they rooted in the earth. It was common for the landowner or Lord of the Manor to receive a pig in return for continuing these rights.

A pig was valued as not only was most of it edible in one form or another, but because when they farrowed they produced relatively large litters, thus they were cheap to buy while their ubiquitous diet made them easy to keep.

Killing the pig was a ritual that is remarked upon in many historical records, in paintings and in folklore. Part of the reason for this is that it often involved the whole community, some as participants, others as observers. In this respect it was a kind of macabre theatre as A.G. Street remarks in his book *Farmer's Glory*: 'The shriek of dying pigs; I hear them still.'

Recalling her childhood in the 1920s, Phyllis Crowson from a small village in Cambridgeshire, leaves a vivid description:

A young pig would be bought either from the local market or from someone in the village who had a breeding sow. This small animal would soon start to grow if fed properly – small potatoes boiled in their skins, mixed with other scraps and barley meal. Pigs were only killed between October and March, the colder the weather the better, and when the pig weighed about 16 stones.

A farmer's wife feeding a piglet from a bottle on a Dartmoor farm in the 1930s.

We had our own pig killer in Helpston, named Butty Chambers. He would arrive at about 8am, complete with a very large tub, knives and meat chopper, all pushed on what looked like an extra long wheelbarrow without sides, know as 'The Scratch'. It was long enough for a large pig to lie on.

After killing, the pig was put into the tub and gallons of very hot water poured over it then scraped all over until all the bristles were removed. It was then strung by its hind legs onto a good stout beam and opened completely from head to tail, the 'bellies' removed – later to be cleaned (a very smelly job) and then used for sausage skins. The pig was then left for several hours for the meat to cool until Butty Chambers returned later in the day. The heart, kidneys, liver, head, lungs (known as leaf fat) were removed and the carcase was jointed into gammon hams, shoulder hams and flitches. These were then put into a large wooden trough (sometimes lead lined) and covered with salt, bought in huge lumps some weeks before, cut up and crushed. The hams were rubbed in the thickest part with salt petre and brown sugar as well as salt to ensure deeper penetration for a good cure, more salt would be added during the next 3 weeks; the flitches were then removed but the hams left for another week. The cured meat was then brushed and lightly washed and dried and either stored, packed in lime, in a large wooden chest or tied up in white bags (like pillow cases, and hung on a wall – hams on beams.

The slaughtered pig lies on a 'scratch' or 'pig bench' in this photograph taken in Probus, Cornwall, in the 1920s. The man on the right has drawn water from the steaming copper which he will pour on to the carcase to soften the bristles. The man on the left holds a knife and steel ready to scrape the bristles from the pig.

The offal taken from the pig was used as follows – some of the liver, melt, brain, kidneys and heart were covered with a veil-like fat, (called caul), and cooked in the oven – this was called 'pigs fry'; part of the head, trotters and most trimmings were made into brawn, the other part of the head was roasted as chaps; the remains of the liver, heart, lights etc were minced and mixed with leeks (never onions as they give the wrong flavour) and made into faggots then covered with caul and baked. Sausage was made from the trimmings of the meat mixed with herbs. The leaf fat (the best in the pig) was cut up and put into a pan to be rendered down to make home cured lard, which was lovely to eat on bread or toast, the remains after the rendering were left to cool and then eaten, known as 'scraps' – they were delicious.

*   *   *

The slaughtered pig is hauled into the barn on a wooden sledge ready to be hefted on to a beam where it will be butchered. Photographed at Sampford Courtenay in Devon in the early 1900s.

As we have seen, the kitchen was the centre of the farming wife's world, the fireplace or range lying at its heart. For every meal bread would be eaten, in earlier times made from flour ground, by law, by the local miller. By the mid 1800s commercially made flour was commonly available and the practice of baking homemade bread was declining as local bakeries made deliveries, first in horse-drawn carts and then in vans. A resident of Probus, Cornwall in the 1920s recalls the family business:

I'm as Cornish as you make 'em! I was born at the bakery in Probus and as soon as Irene and I were old enough, we helped with the business. We only had horses and wagons to deliver in Philleigh, Veryan and Ruan, Grampound Road and Coombe, and as far as New Mills, Ladock, Merther, St Erme and St Michael Penkevil! A hand cart served the village, but later on we had a bright yellow Ford van – a real 'tin lizzie'.

Baking started at four in the morning and the big oven baked 300 loaves at one time. The price was 2¼d. or 4¼d. We made pasties too.

Established in Nottingham in 1885, Coombs' flour mill went on to provide the housewife with a range of baking products 'which render it possible for the person with the weakest digestion to partake of cakes and pastry produced from it without fear of any unpleasant after results'.

Those who persisted with home baking continued to use traditional bread ovens, or the oven of cast iron stoves fired either by solid fuel or oil. Town gas, as it was called, was slowly being made available to rural communities but the cost of laying pipelines meant that the most remote places and individual farms would never have this facility. The thriftiest families continued to make the most of what fuel was readily available to them, much as their medieval ancestors had done for cooking and heating their homes.

While life-threatening poverty and hunger continued to dog the rural poor well into the twentieth century, the increasing mass-production of food and its ready availability through improved transport links and the mushrooming of local shops gradually eased the spectres of starvation and disease that had haunted country people for centuries past.

Cerne Abbas c.1915 and bundles of faggots have been dropped off on the roadside in the front of each of the cottages.

Cleanliness & Godliness

*"Let women be what God intended, a helpmate for man,
but with totally different duties and vocations."*

Queen Victoria (1819–1901)

Queen Victoria reigned for 63 years and 7 months during which time the population of Britain grew from 11.5 million in 1820 to 36 million in 1900. At home the great cities of the industrialised age rose above the green and pleasant land, their factories crammed with labourers formerly tied to the land. Abroad the Empire held sway over one-fifth of the world's population dominated, as George Orwell has it, by 'dull, decent people cherishing and fortifying their dullness behind a quarter of a million bayonets'.

Religion and respectability were behind the ideals of the aspirational middle classes who emerged from the wealth of the Empire, principles that seeped down even to the poorest members of society. Religion was fundamental to the work of many social reformers of the age, their motivation driven as much by morality as by a pragmatic desire to alleviate the suffering of the poor. Evangelists found new work in the missions of the Empire and at home used the cry of 'Christian conscience' to promote social reform. Methodism, always a religion of the poor, grew in strength among rural communities who found its robust practical teachings to their liking; being clean and being godly was a recurring theme, as the nineteenth century hymn has it:

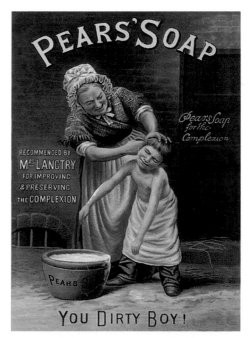

Being clean meant more than being hygienic for the Victorians, and advertisers used this to good effect.

*One thing I of the Lord desire,
For all my path hath miry been,
Be it by water or by fire,
O make me clean, O make me clean.*

Advertisers were, as ever, quick to exploit the mood of the times and late Victorian housewives were confronted by advertisements for cleaning products at every opportunity. Shopfronts, station platforms, horse-drawn omnibuses and any available wall were fair game to bill posters. In a society less cynical than our own, and innocent to the wiles of the advertising world, the messages sent out by the manufacturers of goods aimed at the housewife were extremely effective; those that reinforced the ethical and moral views of the day, doubly so.

The age of advertising. A wall in Torquay, Devon photographed in 1882 carries posters promoting religious events, powdered egg, fat-stock auctions, poultry, 'metallic' mattresses, along with the date for a lecture on 'Land and the Labourer' to be given by the Allotment and Smallholding Association.

Members of the Salvation Army gather in Bridgwater, Somerset c.1900. A Christian organisation, the Army was founded by William Booth and his wife Catherine in 1865 'to bring salvation to the poor, destitute and needy'.

Publishers also jumped on the bandwagon offering practical as well as moral advice aimed at the new generation of housewives, those who had learned to read in school now that education was compulsory, the Elementary Education Act of 1880 making this so for all 5–10 year olds.

One of the earliest and best known of these 'improving' volumes was the aptly named *Self Help: With Illustrations of Conduct and Perseverance* by Samuel Smiles, published in 1859 and aimed at the labouring classes, specifically men, and providing uplifting examples of famous and successful figures who had risen from humble backgrounds. Other books soon followed each offering advice, often in patronising but well-meaning terms as in the 1910 *Practical Suggestions for Mother and Housewife* by Marion Miller:

A house fitted up with clean good furniture, the kitchen provided with clean wholesome-looking cooking utensils, good fires, clean good table-linen, the furniture of the table and sideboard good of the kind without ostentation, and a well-dressed plain dinner, bespeak a sound judgment and correct taste that place the family on a footing of respectability. It is only conforming to our sphere, not vainly attempting to be above it, that can command true respect.

Victorian fantasy and reality. In 'The New Baby' by artist Carlton Alfred Smith (1853–1946) we are presented with a sentimental scene of the young mother sitting beside the cottage fire rocking the cradle of her newborn. Her surroundings are poor but sunlight bathes the room in an optimistic glow. But in reality such poverty could easily result in separation for mother and child with the prospect of confinement in the workhouse. In the photograph above elderly women in the workhouse sit in disciplined silence at their meal – separated from husbands and children. In 1850, railing against the iniquities of the Overseers of the Poor, philanthropist William Rathbone, wrote:

There is grinding want among the honest poor; there is starvation, squalor, misery beyond description, children lack food and mothers work their eyes dim and their bodies to emaciation in the vain attempt to find the bare necessities of life, but the Poor Law authorities have no record of these struggles.

Nowhere was the religious aspect of moral improvement so conflated with the idea of cleanliness and self-improvement than in the parish workhouse. These were places where, under various Poor Law Acts, those unable to support themselves were confined under a rigorous and often cruel regime. By late Victorian times they housed more of the elderly, sick and infirm than of working poor, becoming bywords in stifling discipline and inhumane treatment. For those families already subject to the harshness of agricultural labour, to jobs and homes tied to the vagaries of landowners, the workhouse was a dread prospect. Worse for the mother who threw herself on the mercy of the workhouse was the fact that she would be separated from her children. A report to Parliament recorded in *Hansard* in April 1876 refers specifically to the plight of women:

Not only was the result of the system bad with regard to the children, but it produced the most horrible and frightful feelings in the women themselves. The recklessness of human life by these women was something terrible—nay, almost brutal. Young women were often seduced whilst at their employment, and after coming out of the workhouse they lost their children, and the brutality of elder mothers after losing one or two children was something shocking. It was a common remark of the neighbours, after a woman had had one or two children, for them to say amongst themselves when she had another, "Oh, that won't live long"—the prophecy being made the subject of laughter.

It was against this background that the rural poor in Victoria's reign eked out their daily lives, suffering the constant anxieties associated with poverty, while their better off neighbours were, towards the end of the century, enjoying a life enhanced by more secure employment and higher wages brought about by growing Union strength, state education for their children and access to more secure sources of food.

"Please Sir, I want some more?'. George Cruikshank's illustration for Charles Dickens' Oliver Twist is one of the most enduring images of the Victorian's treatment of the poor. Orphan Oliver's trials in the workhouse as described by the author helped in the movement towards building a more compassionate society.

The Bridgwater Workhouse in Taunton, photographed in 1865. The forbidding aspect of many such buildings did little to dispel their reputation for ill-treatment.

Members of the Spetisbury, Dorset, Girls' Friendly Society shortly after the First World War. The branch had been formed in 1891 under the aims of the Society that all young women, whatever their class, should band together for mutual help. 'No girl who has not borne a virtuous character to be admitted,' was one of their tenets and a distinction was still made between ladies, who were associates, and girls and young women, who were only members. At meetings girls did useful sewing for charity, and listened to biblical readings, and there was a regional annual festival with processions, service and tea. The Society still exists.

Shortly before this photograph was taken, the Women's Institute was formed, in 1915, with one of its specific aims to revitalise rural communities. It remains today as the principal organisation for women in rural areas.

The work of political reformers was matched on the ground by the rise of organisations, often Christian or Socialist in intent, who through concerted efforts aimed to alleviate the concerns of the sick and the poor. The Band of Hope and the Mothers' Union, mentioned earlier, were just two of a swathe of such groups whose charitable work was usually centred upon a local church, chapel or meeting room but organised under a national banner. Among many others, all appearing in the Victorian era, are included: The British Association for the Promotion of Temperance (founded 1835), The Independent Order of Rechabites (1835), The National Temperance Society (1865), The Girls' Friendly Society (1875), The Church Army (1882), The Boys' Brigade (1883) The Girls' Brigade (1893), and The Church Girls' Brigade (1901).

Coinciding with the rise of cheap transport, such groups organised outings in order to maintain the cohesiveness of the organisation and to attract new members. These were particularly popular among rural communities where transport links were poor and the opportunities for holidays or day trips were fewer. More regularly held were Tea Treats in which the members of a particular church or chapel would combine a short religious service with tea, often in the grounds of a vicarage or church, or perhaps at a nearby beauty spot. A record from Cornwall:

On Saturday June 25th 1836 The day appointed for the Tea Drinking, the weather being fine the children walked two and two attended by their teachers to the top of the watch

Members of the Monmouth WI are taught lessons in bottling and pickling in the 1930s.

The Band of Hope tea treat at Carne Hill in Cornwall in 1911. The children are holding up their huge saffron buns for the camera.

Children in High Bickington Devon in the early 1900s. Poverty still stalked rural communities well into the twentieth century and what the more romantic writers might describe as rustic charm was often in reality degrading conditions. The house in the foreground is where Elias and Eva Parker brought up their 15 children.

(a hill so called) which commands a fine prospect of the western part of Cornwall, extending from the Lands End to Redruth. The following hymn was sung on the summits of the Hill, 'I Sing the Almighty Power of God which made the mountains rise' and the 4th verse was particularly striking from the elevated situation of the children and teachers while engaged in singing it.

"Lord how thy wonders are display'd
Where'er I turn my eye
If I survey the ground I tread
Or gaze upon the sky."

At the close of the walk the children were treated to tea and cake and after the children had gone home, the teachers sat down to have their tea and heard an address on the subject of Sabbath schools.

Annual church and chapel outings by charabanc, coach and train remained popular until individual car ownership became commonplace in the 1960s.

*   *   *

Poverty in the countryside was more obscure than urban deprivation. The myth of the 'rural idyll' persisted well into the twentieth century, the picturesque often masking blight that would be more obvious in towns and cities. That it affected fewer people overall meant that politicians could overlook it too.

Members of Great Bedwyns Friendly Society in Wiltshire gather under their banner c.1900. While having some of the aims of Trades Unions the main purpose of 'Sick Clubs' was to serve their immediate community by providing financial help to the families of those in need. Their popularity varied across the country, the census of 1821 estimating that while only 5 per cent of Dorset's population belonged to one or other such mutual associations, in Lancashire this was almost 20 per cent.

Along with church groups, Friendly Societies were established as a form of communal self-help in the days before governments provided health care or benefits for the unemployed. Members of each society (and there were many, variously named) sometimes known as benefit clubs, often had their base in the local pub where members met each month for a social evening at which members paid a small subscription to the society's fund. The payments entitled members to a weekly benefit when ill-health prevented them from working, as well as a lump sum for the family when they died. Such societies, or 'Sick Clubs' as they were popularly known, were governed under the Friendly Societies Act of 1875, and many still survive today. For the wives and children of rural working men the security offered by these clubs was of huge importance, while the comradeship they offered led to formal social gatherings.

In some communities existing charities performed a similar function, providing benefits in money or in kind to those in need. In the late Victorian period it became common for wealthy individuals to start a local fund to pay directly for the services of a district nurse, part of whose role would be to educate mothers into the importance of hygiene in the home in order to prevent disease. As time went on the work of these nurses was incorporated into the National Health System.

Education for country children was often of a lower standard than that in urban schools. Recruitment of trained teachers to rural areas was more difficult while the indifference of parents who thought of 'book learning' as something best avoided undermined the best intentions of the educational authorities. Conditions in late Victorian schools were fairly spartan as Fred Gamble, a Cambridgeshire boy, recalls:

While members of Friendly Societies could rely on payments for health care in times of illness, the availability of trained doctors was patchy. Tried and tested remedies passed down from earlier generations were relied on for many 'cures', while the range of proprietory medicines grew enormously from the mid 1850s. Where a qualified doctor was unavailable people turned to trusted practitioners who had a track record of success. This photograph is of Granny Spargo of Constantine in Cornwall in the 1890s. She was called upon to perform as a midwife locally as well as helping to lay out the dead.

A typical infants' classroom in a Victorian school with low wooden benches and chairs and slates or blackboards for the children to draw on. Here they are threading beads while, for the photographer's benefit, a boy is riding the rocking horse at the back of the class. Before purpose-built schools, classes would be held in church rooms or village halls, spartan in comparison to this classroom.

We had two rooms, a large one for the bigger kids and a small one for the infants. We had long desks so you sat in rows and scratched away on the old slates — and spat on them to clean them. There were a hundred or so of us in the school altogether, although they weren't usually all in at the same time. Like harvest time – they were away helping their parents in the fields, or potato-sowing or hop-picking. On 7 July 1893, the wedding day of the Duke of York, we all had a holiday. And of course they used to close the school down regularly for measles or influenza. Then in the winter you'd get some away if it was raining and storming, or snowing. A mother might keep her child at home if it hadn't got a good pair of well dubbined boots or a warm coat. And even if it did have, it couldn't always get them dry in front of the schoolroom stove: we had those old tortoise stoves with an iron smoke-pipe. Of course in the summer it was so hot and stuffy you couldn't breathe. I reckon the old germs loved it in there. There were no school meals and no water taps. We had to take our own lunches.

Sampford Courtenay Village School in Devon c.1900. There were over 60 pupils with ages ranging from four or five years up to early teens. The headmaster and his wife were supported by a teaching assistant and it was common for older pupils to act as monitors in classrooms, helping youngsters in lessons or reading and writing. Note both boys and girls in the front row wearing huge hobnailed boots.

Religious education was a major part of a school's curriculum with morning assembly hymns and prayers. A school inspector in Worcestershire reports on an infant class: 'They repeat their prayers distinctly, and join in the hymns with others: having also learnt several by themselves.'

School log books from the late 1800s are full of records of the teachers' frustration at farming children always being absent. At Hemyock in Devon the following are among the reasons given for failure to attend: acorn picking, blackberry picking, apple picking, potato digging, haymaking and corn harvesting, rabbiting, the annual ploughing match and sheep shearing. Fines could be imposed on parents for such absences but as a teacher at Bridestowe, also in Devon, records in 1887:

It seems only a farce to send in a list of absentees to the Attendance Officer, as they are not taking the slightest notice of, the same names being continually forwarded month after month.

And absence was not confined to farm work, or to boys, as schoolteacher Miss Webster of Axminster writes in the 1860s:

Thin school, many had gone and four of my best, first-class girls not at school this week. Fear they have left altogether and several of the girls have gone to service and others are obliged to be kept at home to help mothers. Parents are anxious for their girls to do as much needlework as they can.

A school certificate for passing the sixth grade presented to Matilda Harris in 1889.

A domestic science class at Haughley School, Suffolk, in 1940. It was to be some years before boys were considered for these lessons as a matter of course.

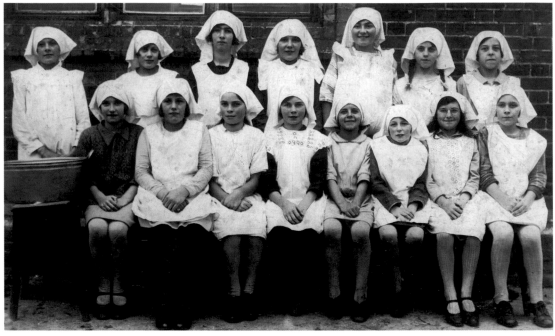

A Cumbrian housewife at her washing tub. In her left hand she holds a washboard against which the clothes would be held to be scrubbed. Beside her stands the washing dolly peg used to agitate the clothes in the dolly tub – the barrel – when filled with soapy water.

As late as the 1950s many small village schools were still lagging some way behind the requirements of the national curriculum. A friend of the author's recalls that in North Bovey School in Devon one of the main lessons for the boys was gardening and for the girls sewing and cooking. If the weather was fine teachers, girls and boys would spend the day on long country walks!

*   *   *

In all this the farming wife would have the daily responsibility in caring for her children, in clothing and feeding them sufficient for a day at school, and no doubt providing the buffer between the frustrations of the teacher and the needs of her farmer husband. Yet, if hard work truly is the road to salvation, as Samuel Smiles suggested, then the farmer's wife was already assured of a place in heaven; and in returning to the theme of this chapter we end it with a brief look at clothes washing.

Washing day lasted all day; the water had to be carried from the pump and heated in the boiler, then the clothes were washed, then boiled, then steamed, next they were put in a bath of cold water with Reckitts Blue. The only soap was Hudson's Powder and soda was also used. It was real hard work. The old wooden roller mangle was kept outside the door as it was too big to come inside. I can still recall having to stand out there on a bitter cold day and get all that washing through that old wringer.

Washing day at Sticker in Cornwall, 1910. Mechanical mangles or wringers, such as that the women in the photograph are using, and which squeezed out the water after washing, were formerly used by professional laundrywomen as they were too expensive for domestic purposes. However, by the end of the nineteenth century they became more affordable, often fitted with rubber rollers instead of wood.

In medieval times washing clothes, where it was done at all, was a communal affair, women meeting down at the pond or on the riverbank to wash clothes just as it is still done today in the Third World. In some medieval towns they built wash houses close to a supply of running water for communal clothes washing. In 1846 The Public Baths and Wash Houses Act allowed local parishes to raise money to provide public baths and laundries. Women in the workhouse were also obliged to wash laundry taken in by the workhouse master.

In the countryside it had long been the case that one or two women in a village would take in washing for the community and this became more common during the late nineteenth and early twentieth centuries. Winifred Farley of Kingskerswell in Devon remembers:

My mother and grandmother had a laundry in the village. Clothes were collected from the big houses in the village, and our mother took over the starching and pressing of fine linen and lace. The laundry was then delivered back to the houses by all three of them.

On sunny days the washing would be draped around the village, either laid on bushes in gardens and fields, or more conventionally on washing lines strung between poles.

Drying day at a cottage laundry in Hether-settt, Norfolk c.1910.

The outside wash house was a 'modern' convenience in Victorian farms and cottages where clothes washing facilities were kept separate from the house. Here Annie Porter at Lower Green Farm, Hindringham, chops wood to fire the boiler, the chimney for which rises above the wash house roof, water for the boiler being dipped from the rainwater barrel.

Monday was traditionally washing day in households throughout Britain and there are those still for whom Monday will forever be tainted with the smell of damp washing. A Derbyshire woman recalls her mother's weekly round as it happened in the early years of the twentieth century:

Monday*: wash day, all day, rubbing clothes on the washing board, dolly pegging and mangling. It was all really hard work. In time, we progressed from dolly pegging to a copper posser in the dolly tub. We had a set boiler built into a corner of the kitchen, like most folk. You had to be up early to light the fire under it, to heat your water. When you had boiled the clothes and rinsed them, they had to be blued. You had to put a bit of starch in with the blue. It was all day of a job, you know, washing.*
Tuesday: *ironing. The clothes that you didn't iron were put through the mangle again. Of course, you used a flat iron, which had to be warmed on the hob.*
Wednesday: *upstairs cleaning. It was a day's job as well, mopping and polishing everywhere. Most folk had children at home and meals to look to as well.*
Thursday: *baking day. My mother did all her cooking on a large range – most folk did. Mother always made her own bread, pastry, cakes and everything. She would be baking all day on Thursday. She used to make tea cakes as well. I loved coming home from school on baking days – the house was full of wonderful smells.*

Friday: *downstairs cleaning day; everything shined and polished for the weekend. We had an order from the Co-op; it came on Fridays, so the order had to be put away.*
Saturday: *we got everything ready for Sundays.*
Sunday: *church and chapel.*

*   *   *

Personal cleanliness and its spiritual connections can be found in many religions, not least in the practice of baptism. From the eponymous St John to the present day the idea of being clean in body and in mind are literally ingrained in our culture. From a purely practical point of view the Romans provided succeeding civilizations with all the lessons needed in the art of bathing, an education not always heeded by those living through the Dark Ages, and beyond.

Above: Raising water from the well at Treen in Cornwall c.1890.

Below: A little girl collects water at The Lady Well, Sticklepath in Devon, early 1900s.

Medieval nobility took baths infrequently. They washed their hands before meals, more in ritual than for hygiene, using scented oils and perfumes. Priests warned the peasantry that immersing the naked body in water somehow let in the devil, though during outbreaks of the plague washing was recommended to keep the evil humours at bay.

The Victorian passion for self-improvement combined with improvements in household sanitation sowed the seeds from which contemporary faddish abluting spring. Theirs was the age of disinfecting, polishing and sweeping, in which the housewife's (or her maid's) care of the person and the household became paramount, and manufacturers were busily making and selling every possible aid and device to achieve this.

Newfangled notions were often adopted rather more slowly in the countryside; a single tap bringing cold water into the house was considered luxury and only by the 1940s would this have been thought primitive. Other sanitary arrangements on many farms, such as the family water closet, remained spartan more than half a century after Thomas Crapper patented his own syphon toilet system in the 1880s. In recollecting her childhood in the 1930s, Marian Dummett of Cullompton in Devon relates:

Lucifer in the loo – a graphic lesson in cleanliness and godliness. John Harington is said to have been the inventor of the flush toilet. In his 1596 book A new discourse on a stale subject, called the metamorphosis of Ajax *(a play on the word jakes, being an old name for a water closet), the author refutes the accusation that sitting contemplatively on the toilet seat was ungodly. On the contrary he retorts to the devil:*

"To God my prayer I meant, to thee the durt
Pure prayr ascends to him that high doth sit
Down fals the filth, for fiends of hel more fit."

Miss Hunt in 1890 at Foxworthy Farm on Dartmoor washing vegetables at the outside granite trough into which ran the farmhouse domestic water supply.

Our toilet at that time was a bucket in the lavatory round the back of the house. The contents would be buried in the garden when necessary. Another job for children was to tear up newspaper, the Daily Herald, *into little squares and thread them onto string for toilet paper! Baths were in the shed in the summer and by the living room fire on a Saturday night in the winter. Hot water had to come from the coal range which had to be lit every day before we could have a cup of tea or hot water to wash. Went out to the woods with an old pram to pick up bigger sticks for the fire.*

Jan Humphreys, a resident of Kingskerwell in Devon confirms that even as late as the 1950s some country folk's living conditions had hardly changed from those of the Victorian era:

Above: A maid empties ash from the domestic fireplace through a series of screens into the bucket of an outside water closet in order to reduce odours and make collection of the 'night soil' easier.

Below: Victorian advertisement for a washstand

Now my grandfather's house was quite old-fashioned; they did not have hot running water or electric lights. There was a gas mantle in the kitchen and hallway, and that was all. If you wanted to go to the toilet, it was down the back stairs and outside. The toilet had a huge wooden seat which was scrubbed every Monday after the washing was done, and no modern toilet paper – it was newspaper hung on a skewer. It was so cold to go down there in the winter. If you wanted to go to toilet in the middle of the night, you used a pail or pot. Then in the morning you went and emptied it. At night you took your candle with you upstairs. If it was winter, also a hot-water bottle, which doubled as your water in the morning to wash with.

The washstand became a fixture in the bedrooms of farms and cottages, comprising a marble top into which was set a removable china bowl, with a complementing water jug and soap dish. This equipment and the chamber pot under the bed completed toilet arrangements in the 'modern' rural household.

Deal Washstand, very strong,
painted Oak or Maple.

A saucy Edwardian postcard dated 1909 on which the message read 'I saw you at Whitby but I couldn't see your face.'

It is difficult to argue against the popular notion that country people, farmers in particular, have a more pragmatic approach to sex and sexual behaviour, being daily witness to the animals in their care doing what comes naturally. Certainly the view of the Victorian's attitude to sex as being something they recoiled from is refuted by modern historians who suggest many couples seem to have enjoyed mutual pleasure in what is now seen as a normal, modern manner.

What was different was the high mortality rate among mothers in childbirth and among newly born children, the uncertainty of contraceptive methods and the insecurity that all this brought to those wishing to establish a family. Traditionally this had led to large families although there is plain evidence that the early Victorian family of six to eight or more children was on its way out by 1900.

According to a report *Happy Families*, published by the British Academy in 2011, between the 1770s and the mid nineteenth century the average number of children born per woman was around six. From the 1870s the number fell gradually to an average of two by the 1930s. In the early nineteenth century an estimated 20 percent of first births were 'illegitimate' and over half of all first births were probably conceived outside marriage. This suggests that premarital sex was a normal part of the courtship process, from at least the mid eighteenth century.

As if farmwork were not enough, the care of a new baby fell on the other children as much as on the mother. Victorian school reports are littered with references to absences while a pupil was held at home to care for a brother or sister. For those children that did survive, a happy life, though not guaranteed, often lay ahead.

Baby Dorrie sits among the pigs.

122

The Pioneer Wife

Circles of white-tented wagons may now be seen in every direction, and the smoke from campfires is circling upwards, morning noon and evening. Parties of Indians, hunters and emigrants are galloping to and fro. It is difficult to realize we are in a wilderness, a thousand miles from civilization.

Edwin Bryant, emigrant 1846

Nowhere are the qualities of the farming wife displayed to better advantage than in the resourcefulness shown by those who emigrated. Driven by economic depression, despair at the exploits of successive governments, the promise of a better life, or simply by a sense of adventure, the pioneers set off for foreign shores often with little idea of what lay ahead. In the late 1800s small farmers, farm labourers and their families were suffering most acutely. The population explosion had given a fillip to grain production, and grain could be grown more profitably on large farms than on small ones; larger ones also requiring fewer labourers.

Population figures in the last half of the nineteenth century give some idea of the enormous social upheaval of the time. Between 1851 and 1901 the population of England more than doubled from 16.8 million to around 36 million. In the same

A poster published in 1839 inviting would-be emigrants to attend a lecture 'for the instruction of the WORKING CLASSES' encouraging them to leave for Australia.

A John Leech cartoon titled 'Here and There; or Emigration a remedy,' published in 1848. On the left is a destitute husband and wife with their starving children, on the right the same family enjoying the bounties of their new home abroad.

123

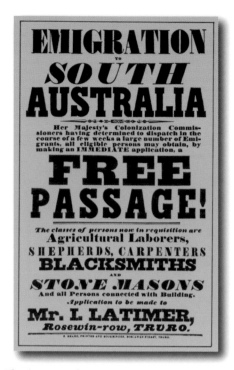

The impetus for emigration came from two directions: poverty and overcrowding at home and the promotion of a better life in the new lands. That in some instances it cost little to make the journey was an added incentive.

While the new colonies and the authorities in the United States were desperate for skilled labour, the emigrants were by no means restricted to single men and married men and their families. Single women were in great demand too, not least as eligible wives for those men who had already settled abroad. This is the scene in a female emigrants' home in England in 1853 where single women awaited departure by ship.

It would be tempting to suggest that with these pioneers went the best of Britain's enterprising women, although we also know that the emigrant boats were also full of criminals, near-criminals, dead beats and chancers. What is certainly true is that those women who remained at home cast envious glances in the direction of those who wrote to say they had indeed found 'a land of the free'.

period Scotland's population also rose rapidly from 2.8 million in 1851 to 4.4 million. Ireland's population decreased from 8.2 million in 1841 to less than 4.5 million in 1901, mostly due to the Great Famine. In the same period a staggering 15 million emigrants left the United Kingdom, most of them heading for the United States, Canada, and Australia.

In the centuries prior to this, other than religious colonists, emigration had been piecemeal, individuals and small parties travelling to undertake specific roles in the new worlds. Other migrants had no choice but to go, these being transportees who for a variety of crimes spent their sentences in foreign climes. We touch upon the topic of transportation here only insofar as many of the convicts sent abroad were country people forced into a life of crime by dire need. From around 1780 to 1840 over 150 000 prisoners were transported to Australia, many of them for the most petty of crimes: In 1789 Ann Marsh aged 22 was convicted of stealing a bushel of wheat and sentenced to be transported. In 1801 Robert Weeks received a life sentence and was transported for stealing sheep. In 1803 Elizabeth Banfield was sentenced for 7 years for stealing sugar. In 1820 John Frazer was sentenced to 7 years for theft of a silk handkerchief. In 1821 Martha Brooke was sentenced for 14 years for stealing bread and breaking into a dairy. Such was the desperation of the poor and the harshness of the treatment they received at the hands of the law.

Transportation to the Americas ended with the War of Independence in 1873 and to Australia in the 1840s. Now the colonies and the United States wanted free and honest labour to exploit their new lands and they did their utmost to attract immigrants to come. Shipping companies vied with each other to offer the most attractive fares, with free passage offered by the Australian Commissioners. In the US this led to 'Boosterism' as those with vested interests made extravagant predictions for the lives of new settlers. Territories competed with each other, producing advertisements and books aimed at attracting would-be emigrants to their particular 'Arcadia'. The text of one such, hoping to attract settlers to Oregon, read:

In this country all is superceded by Nature's own beautiful hand. In this country a single shepherd with his horse and dogs can protect and look after 5000 sheep. A man with his horse and perhaps a dog can easily attend to 2000 head of cattle and horses, without spending a dollar for barns, grain or hay. Were I to select for my friends a location for a healthy, happy and speedy wealth, this would be the country.

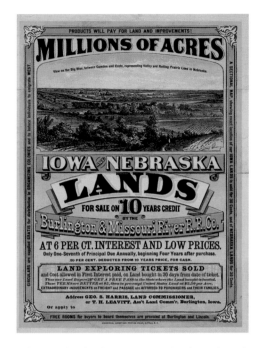

Those who had most to gain from immigrants pouring in to the United States, the government officials and landowners, employed a number of tactics to convince travellers that their particular region offered the best opportunities. 'Boosters' were employed to write books and pamphlets extolling the virtues of settlement in particular places and cheap, or free, land on offer was irresistible to many farming families taken in by the hyperbole. The real lie of the land once they arrived after a long and arduous journey was often quite different to how it had been described and how they had imagined it to be.

In 1862 the US Government pushed through the Homestead Act which originally gave an opportunity to claim at little or no cost a grant of land of 160 acres, and the flood gates were well and truly opened. From around 18 000 emigrants leaving the UK for North America in 1821, in 1891 this figure reached just short of 300 000.

In their book *Ever Westward the Land*, authors A.C. Todd and David James describe the trials of a Cornish farmer and his family who in 1842 leave their home to undertake the archetypal emigrant journey across America on the Oregon Trail. The party comprised Samuel James, his wife Anna Maria, and their four sons, the eldest being only 8 years old. Sick of life in 'the House of Bondage' Samuel wrote that he now looked forward to a life 'in the land of freedom'.

Their journey began in April 1842 on the emigrant ship *Orient* sailing from the port of Falmouth, Anna Maria, aged 36 and six months pregnant, sailing ahead with the two youngest boys, Thomas aged three and John Rogers not yet two, while Samuel tied up loose ends on the sale of their Cornish farm.

The vessel seemed barely seaworthy, its master praying audibly for 'one last safe voyage' and the crossing in high winds and heavy seas frightful. Life below deck was appalling, the stench of vomit everywhere, as Anna Maria comforted her terrified children.

Samuel and his two eldest sons eventually joined Anna Maria in Wisconsin, now with her new child, a daughter Anna Eliza. But Samuel grew restless in their new home and by 1850 he determined to head West, in part encouraged by the writing of an earlier pioneer Jesse Quinn Thornton whose published diaries, *Oregon and California in 1848* inspired many others to take the Oregon Trail.

Pioneers on the trail. Note the women are wearing traditional bonnets as seen in photographs elsewhere in this book, also that they are smoking clay pipes. Habits were changed by the exigencies of the journey, as one commentator observed:

'Of the fortitude of the women one cannot say too much. Embarrassed at the start by the follies of fashion, they soon rose to the occasion and cast false modesty aside. Long dresses were quickly discarded and the bloomer donned. Could we but have had the camera trained on one of these typical camps, what a picture there would be. Elderly matrons dressed almost like little girls of today. The younger women were rather shy in accepting the inevitable but finally fell into the procession, and soon we had a community of women wearing bloomers. Some of them went barefoot, partly from choice and in some cases from necessity.'

Artist William Bierstadt's 1867 painting 'Emigrants Crossing the Plains' literally casts a rosy glow over the event. The reality for most pioneers was somewhat different.

And so, in October 1850, the family packed all their possessions into three covered wagons, each pulled by a yoke of three oxen, and set off along with their small herd of cows on the 2000 mile journey across America. As with the 400 000 other settlers, ranchers, miners and farmers who followed the trail during its 40 years of operation before the railroad took its place, the family and their fellow migrants endured the daily grind of trudging hour by hour across an unforgiving landscape. The dust cloud thrown up by the wagon train was a constant irritant, adding misery to the creaking armada as it crossed the endless plains.

Sickness dogged the children and constant injuries to the men had to be cared for with whatever came to hand, as a later immigrant, Diana Block, recalled:

He had a terrible wound on his hand. It looked as though half his thumb had been shot off, but he said he had done it with his knife. He wanted me to bandage it for him. I started to wrap it with a clean white cloth when he told me to put something on it so the bandage would not stick. I told him I didn't have anything to use. He said, "go and get some axle grease." He took the grease and rubbed it all over his hand. When I was through bandaging it and started to tie it up, he said, "don't tie it - I want you to sew it on so it can't come off." When I came back with a needle and black thread, he said, "No - get some white thread." I told him it was the black thread or none at all, because that's all I had. I sewed it on good and tight.

*   *   *

Anna Maria oversaw the feeding of the family, eking out the rations of flour and dried bacon that formed the bulk of their diet, supplemented by hard tack biscuits. They also carried sacks of coffee, sugar, dried fruit, rice, beans and peas.

Providing nourishing and varied meals was one of the great challenges faced by women on the trail and long days meant wives and mothers got less sleep than the men. Their day started at 4.00am, an hour before the men rose, in order to cook breakfast and ended after dark clearing up after supper. Their chores were often thwarted by inadequate ovens, cooking vessels that got cracked by the jolting wagons and rain that put out the fires.

For some the journey proved fatal, others discarded most of their possessions in order to lighten the load on their wearied animals and those coming after simply followed a trail of jettisoned goods. Lucky escapes are a common part of the pioneering story, and it's here worth relating another episode of Diana Block's reminiscences:

The first part of our trip had gone pretty smoothly. But by November we had nothing more to sell. We were out of money and our food supply was nearly gone. It had been a long time since we passed through the last settlement and we had seen no one. We were worried. It was getting cold, and we were hitting some of the early winter storms. To make matters worse Mrs Davis was ailing, we knew her baby could come at any time. Then came help... one day a cowboy rode into camp, right away he could see what a bad fix we were in. He told us he was working for a big ranch that was about five or six days travel ahead of us; he was sure they would help us out.

We have just started out again when Mrs Davis went into labor. She had a long hard confinement with nothing to help her. To make matters worse we were even low on water. It was the first baby I had ever helped deliver. It was a bad experience for me – one I have never forgotten. We knew Mrs Davis needed a day or so to rest but we were afraid to wait. All we had left was some flour and very little of that, so we kept going.

Along with the family bible, pioneers carried books such as Dr Chase's Recipes, a book that sold through endless editions, in all selling over three-quarters of a million copies. The 1866 edition contained over 800 recipes, everything from making cream soda to curing cancer.

Dust, lack of food and fresh water and the danger of attack from indians were daily part of the concerns for the pioneers on the Oregon Trail. The urgency to press on, driven by a need to reach the Rocky Mountains before snowfall blocked their path, and the simple urge that all felt not to prolong the five-month long journey more than absolutely necessary meant there were few stops, even for the dangerously ill or those about to give birth.

THE FARMER'S WIFE

One of the most hated tasks of the women was the collection of fuel for their fires, particularly buffalo 'chips', the dung from the huge herds that roamed the plains. When dried these made excellent fuel but had a pungent smell and rattlesnakes had a habit of sleeping among the chips.

When we finally reached the ranch, two or three days later, we were in a mighty bad way. After we set up our camp, papa and Mr Davis went to the house to ask for help. The foreman told them they did not have supplies to give us. Papa was heartsick, he knew we couldn't make it to Santa Rosa without help. He hated to come back to camp and tell me the sad news. But papa didn't know we had callers while he was gone. A bunch of the cowboys had seen our camp and stopped to see what we were doing there.

Something told me to show them our tiny baby. They were amazed and crowded in to see it. It was the first newborn baby some of them had ever seen. They left before papa and Mr Davis came back.

That evening we were sitting around our campfire trying to console each other, trying to find a way, when we saw a group of people coming to our camp. I believe it was every ranch hand on the place. The men who had been in our camp that afternoon had spread the story of our little newborn baby. When the foreman heard, he filled two big barrels with grub and was bringing it to us. They all wanted to see the baby. Once again I brought it from the wagon and they all crowded around to see. We stayed there a couple of days, then we traveled on. We still had a long way to go. The baby died three months later.

A group of Mormon pioneers resting on the covered wagons. In 1844 the Mormons followed their leader Brigham Young to what would become their new home in Utah. Many of their fellow Latter Day Saints, unable to afford oxen and wagons, carried all their belonging on handcarts. One such was Alice Parker who was born in Accrington, Lancashire. In 1856, aged 10, Alice, her mother and father, two brothers and a sister, joined a handcart company in Iowa City en route to Salt Lake City. Within a few days her father fell ill and it was left to Alice and her mother to push the cart. When they reached the head of the Salt Lake Valley in September, 1856, Ann collapsed from exhaustion and went no further until a passing carriage pulled the cart into the city. They had walked thirteen hundred miles.

Often short of fresh food, women also made the most of collecting wild berries en route, quickly learning which of these unfamiliar fruits were edible. They were also alive to the dangers of contaminated water and the water retrieved from sinks and hollows along the trail. Heavily alkaline water caused severe sickness among the travellers and water polluted with bison urine and other organisms brought on dysentery and cholera. The need to boil all such water simply added to the toll on the women safeguarding their family's health. And if all that were not enough, even the insects proved oppressive, as pioneer Lydia Miller records:

To add to our misery we ran into a swam of buffalo gnats. We had previously met a train of people whose faces looked as though they had the smallpox. We soon found out it was not the smallpox but the buffalo gnat bites. After I had received several bites I had to cover my head with a blanket till we had passed the swarm for the gnats were so poisonous that each bite raised a large boil on my face and made me very ill.

The need to wash clothes in order to maintain a semblance of civilised living caused friction among the travellers with men reluctant to make the necessary stop for this

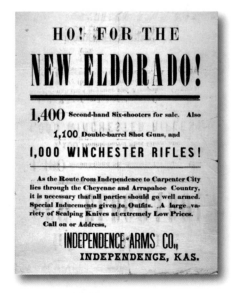

A poster reminded emigrants that they were entering hostile territory and now was the chance to buy arms.

to be done. The tradition of Monday washing was often put aside and the women were obliged to spend Sunday (when the wagons halted for religious services) taking on the back-breaking work, without of course the aid of soap or running water.

Worse, for the more genteel families on the trail, was the behaviour of single men whose course language and boorish behaviour had to be tolerated. Added to this was the lack of privacy for women to undertake personal hygiene and the usual acts of nature. As one diarist records: 'The animal and human excrement that littered the trail was a constant injury to women's habits'.

But nothing created more fear among the women and children than rumours of hostile indians. Having witnessed these massed migrations across their land, the driving away of the buffalo herds on which the tribes depended, the native Americans had every reason to demand something back from the pioneers. But with language and cultural disparities being literally worlds apart there was little hope of reconciling these differences. Constant begging by natives following the wagons and raids to drive off the pioneers' animals were irritants, although outright attacks on the wagon trains were rare. For the women the threat of death, or a fate 'worse then death' was a major preoccupation not least due to the numbers of white women and children who, for whatever reason, were found to be living with the tribes. Lydia Miller again:

One evening, several of us women walked by an Indian camp and saw a little white girl, about 2 years old, with a group of squaws. She was the cutest little thing, wearing a pink sunbonnet, and we figured she probably had been taken during a battle with the whites. Although the Indians were making a treaty, we were advised to hurry out of the Sioux territory as quickly as possible. They said to Captain Cox, "Get these people out of here as fast as you can. Stop only long enough for breakfast and supper." The captain surely knew how to follow orders. We cooked only two meals, breakfast and supper. We didn't stop from the time we broke camp in the morning until night, and continued this way for six weeks. In all that time we weren't even able to wash our clothes. It certainly was terrible.

*   *   *

Cornishman Samuel James and his family survived close encounters with the natives and endured the rigours of the trail, eventually settling in Grand Mound, Washington, in 1852. Here, along with many other pioneers, they cleared and fenced the virgin territory, built a farm and lived out their days in contentment.

Yet the struggle was not over for the farmers who settled the New World. While the idealised Boosters' descriptions of rolling prairie lands ripe for farming sometimes matched the reality, the techniques of farming brought from the Old World and the Continent's climatic extremes were to bring disaster upon the heads of many.

Travellers to the New World carried with them lurid stories of the savagery of native Americans and in particular the raping and scalping of white women. No such story endured longer in the British minds than that of Jane McCrea, fiancé to David Jones, a Loyalist soldier fighting in the War of Independence. In 1777, en route to meet Jones and under escort by Wyandot indians in the employ of the British, McCrea was murdered and scalped. Whatever the true story, news of the outrage was circulated widely in Britain and McCrea's name became a watchword for the fate that awaited women in the New World. 'The Death of Jane McCrea' was painted in 1804 by John Vanderlyn.

THE PIONEER WIFE

One of the most remarkable written and visual records of Britons leaving home to farm in America is left to us through the diaries and photographs of Evelyn Cameron now published in Donna M. Lucey's book *Photographing Montana 1894–1928*. The book tells the story of how, in 1889, newly-married Evelyn and her husband, Ewen, both from genteel backgrounds leave Britain to settle as homesteaders in Montana. Eventually running short of money due to a somewhat feckless husband, Evelyn turned to photography as a way of supplementing the family income and it is through this legacy we are given a vivid portrait of a truly resourceful women pioneer.

Her experience is that of many settlers who fell in love with the freedom and space of the untamed lands of North America but whose dreams of peacefully farming the land were blighted. Few coming from the tiny island of Britain, the total land area of which is less than that of the State of Wyoming alone, with its mild climate and gentle landscape, could conceive of the extremes of weather in the Mountain States.

Encouraged by the opening of the railroads and the development of new strains of wheat, farmers in the early 1900s enjoyed something of a boom, one farmer remarking that Montana was 'destined to be the last and greatest grain garden of the world'. Demand for grain created by the Great War between 1914–18 increased, but as soon as the war ended prices plummeted, while drought and plagues of locusts saw over 20 000 mortgages foreclosed.

Evelyn Cameron kneading dough in the kitchen of her Montana home in 1904. So that her family back in England might get a glimpse of homestead life Evelyn took a number of photographs of herself at work which she then sent to them.

An Evelyn Cameron photograph of a tiny homestead cabin on the Montana plains. Few images could provide so telling a picture of the austere lives of these pioneers. Home for this couple comprised a few sticks of furniture and a single room shack.

An Evelyn Cameron photograph of a log house in Montana in 1909. Resourcefulness was a watchword of these homesteaders who looked to make use of everything that came to hand. The front door is made from parts of a wooden crate, the roof is made from turf sods dug from the prairie. Note also the sheep's familiarity with the family members to whom every animal was precious.

Worse was to come in the 1930s when prolonged drought, combined with extensive deep ploughing of the thin topsoils of the prairie, saw the farmers' land blown away in giant storms that obscured the sun, turning day to night. The Great Dust Bowl affected 100 million acres of land leaving half a million people homeless. Banks foreclosed on hundreds, other farmers simply walked away. The age of the pioneer was swept away with the clouds of dust.

Dust to dust. A South Dakota farmstead lies buried under feet of sand blown by the great dust storm of 1936.

Rebels or Slaves?

I know that women, once convinced that they are doing what is right, that their rebellion is just, will go on, no matter what the difficulties, no matter what the dangers, so long as there is a woman alive to hold up the flag of rebellion. I would rather be a rebel than a slave.

Emmeline Pankhurst

The First World War is rightly described by historians as a pivotal point from which a world that once seemed so immutable was changed forever. Yet the war itself can also be seen as the eye of a storm, a hiatus in which the impending social revolution was put on hold for four years as those who fomented change set aside their demands and aspirations for the duration.

The transition from a farming to an industrialised economy arising from the Industrial Revolution, the rise of the Chartist movement and Trades Unions all combined to unsettle the political and social landscape of Victorian Britain. The 1867 Reform Act finally enfranchised the majority of the male working classes but women still had no vote. Around this time the Irish Home Rule movement became the overriding issue for the people of Ireland and for British political leaders. Various Bills were introduced in the House of Commons during

A call to arms for Irishmen to enlist to fight in the First World War, a conflict that put on hold the Home Rule Act of 1914. Tens of thousands of Irish volunteers joined the British army for the duration.

Left: Police manhandle a suffragette protesting outside Buckingham Palace early in 1914. It was a favourite tactic for women to chain themselves to the railings outside the palace.

133

In the decade before the outbreak of war working people discovered a new strength in collective action. At the William Clowes printing works at Beccles in June 1914, just weeks before the outbreak of war, there was a strike. Although the workers did not belong to a union they refused to work after the factory owner stopped their wages when some of the apprentices took time off to attend a manager's funeral. They eventually returned to work and many then joined a union having secured higher wages. Note the equal numbers of men and women who were engaged in the strike.

the late nineteenth and early twentieth centuries intended to grant self-government but the third such Bill, enacted as the Government of Ireland Act 1914, was suspended on the eve of war.

For women, particularly those of the educated middle classes, it was the right to vote that became the major issue in the decades leading up to the Great War and, again, it was the outbreak of war that postponed much of the campaigning for those calling for women's suffrage.

Thus we can see that it was not just the devastating consequences of the war itself that changed the world, but those four years of conflict that created caesura in the pressure for social change; the weight of water building up behind the dam.

* * *

REBELS OR SLAVES?

The nineteenth-century seeds of working class discontent that lay in the inequalities between the social classes found a voice in the Union movement and in Women's Suffrage. At the outbreak of the First World War the confidence of working people in opposing the establishment had grown. Such unrest was suppressed during the war years only to erupt in furious and violent unrest during the General Strike in 1926.

Trades Unionism was by no means the sole preserve of men, although with women making up only 18 per cent of the total workforce in Britain in 1900, the union movement was inevitably male dominated. Nor were all women in favour of gaining the vote, particularly those of a more conservative nature perhaps living some distance from the towns and cities where political activism was more commonplace.

At the end of Victoria's reign in 1901 many women, despite having few rights, still believed that it was their place to stay at home and look after the needs of their husbands and children. There was no expectation in marriageable young women to seek employment, indeed not being married by a relatively young age was a mark of failure of womanhood. It was to these women that those who opposed the suffrage movement made their appeals, and organisations such as the Women's National Anti-Suffrage League and the National League for Opposing Woman Suffrage, produced pamphlets with titles such as 'Facts versus fancies on woman suffrage' and 'Women's emancipation by one who doesn't want it'. Most men also preferred the status quo.

But such opponents were swimming against the tide. The 1890s had seen a rise in women's trade union membership and the creation of several new women's organi-

Advances in technology and communications brought new opportunities into the lives of the working class women. An improved postal service and telegraph saw offices spring up in almost every village in the country and many women took on the role of local postmistress, as here at Bourton on the Hill in 1910.

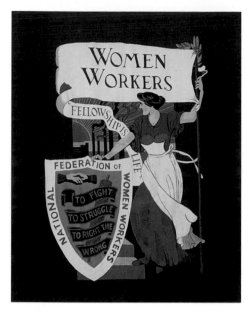

A banner of the National Federation of Women Workers which was formed in 1906. The Federation had close links with the Women's Trade Union League and probably did more than any other organisation (including trade unions) to unionise women, especially during the period of major strikes between 1910–1914.

Lady Drake's maids at Nutwell Court in Devon c.1900. Going into service was often the only option open to young girls from poor country homes, a life of drudgery and servitude for many, as one recalls:

'When I first went out to service I was twelve. I cried when I had to tie my hair up in a bun like a little old woman. My missus was a parson's wife. She'd begrudge us maids even an extra piece of bread. Our food was leftovers. When they had visitors the missus would count every potato to make sure us didn't help ourselves to any.'

sations. The Women's Trade Union Association (WTUA) was founded in 1889, an offshoot of the Women's Trade Union League, itself merging in 1897 with the Women's Industrial Council. In 1870, some 58 000 women were members of trade unions but by 1896 that has risen to 118 000, a figure representing some 7.8 per cent of all union members. By 1914 10 per cent of the total British workforce were women.

For farmers, their wives and families, much of this unrest passed them by. Not so for many farm labourers whose lives still remained at the beck and call of landowners. In E. W. Martin's study of rural life in Devon, *The Shearers and the Shorn* he refers to the age old 'forces which uplifted the rich and depressed the poor', forces which persisted in the countryside well into the twentieth century. This pyramidal hierarchy, based on an unwritten social code, with the landed families at its apex, landowners, the clergy, military personnel and professionals each securing their place on the social ladder, kept the farm labourer firmly at the pyramid's base. Martin records the memories of an old lady who recalls from her childhood in the late 1800s being made to make a little bob whenever they met their 'betters' – 'a bending of the knee, a public confession of inferiority':

When I was small the master would tell father if we didn't make our curtsey. Sometimes we'd pass him or his missus with our noses in the air... The farmer would tell father that he didn't mind for himself. What he wanted was to make sure us poor children were brought up to respect their betters.

Such manners were part of the customs that the socialist movements meant to sweep away, by force if necessary, and in other parts of Europe this is just what happened. Farm labourers were among the growing number of the working class who determined no longer to touch their caps to the bosses, but again the Great War intervened and diverted those who might otherwise have sought conflict on British soil, to fight instead in Flanders fields. Nor was patriotism the principal cause for many to enlist as Ronald Blythe records in *Akenfield*:

> *It must seem there was a war between farmers and their men in those days. These employers were famous for their meanness. They took all they could from the men and boys who worked the land. They bought their life's strength for as little as they could. Fourteen young men left the village in 1909-11 to join the army. There wasn't a recruiting drive, they just escaped.*

With former certainties crumbling, traditions falling to dust and a new order demanded by the downtrodden, this is the context in which the wives of farming men faced the headlong rush to war in August 1914. And while in the public consciousness

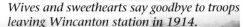

Wives and sweethearts say goodbye to troops leaving Wincanton station in 1914.

today we envisage scenes of women waving cheerily as their men went off to war, this was not always matched by experience, as Mary Stocks records in August 1914:

But though accepted as inevitable, the outbreak of the First World War was not accepted with pleasurable enthusiasm. On the day after the declaration, when mobilization was in full swing, I did a slow cross country rail journey via Birmingham and Westbury to Bridport. At every station there were crowds; but they were unhappy, bewildered apprehensive crowds. I saw no flags waved.

Many of the men employed in agriculture were exempt from military service but joined up anyway, happy for an excuse to leave their dull work behind, not knowing of course what lay ahead. With them went hundreds of thousands of farm horses, requisitioned by the military, a loss to farmers that ultimately changed the face of the countryside forever, as described in my book *Goodbye Old Friend*.

Soldiers' and sailors' wives were compensated for the loss of their husbands through the payment of separation allowances, a reasonably generous sum as the government saw this as an aid to recruitment in an army that was yet voluntary, not conscripted. Paid directly to the wife, voices were raised that this would encourage frivolous spending, the inference being that a woman alone would lack the necessary discipline to control the household budget. The authorities countered by pointing out that any infidelity or misbehaviour was grounds for the removal of the benefit.

Whatever the response of individual women to the circumstances brought about by war, few would have foreseen the fruitless loss of millions of men as being a major springboard in the emancipation of women.

Women munition workers at a factory in Addiscombe c.1915 where they are assembling fuses for artillery shells.

The mass mobilization required by total warfare brought, for the first time, the whole nation into the war effort. As men were recruited into the armed forces so women were brought in to fill those vacancies. While not all women were new to the world of waged work, here necessity called on every able-bodied adult to contribute to the war effort. Being the first truly industrialised war this brought thousands of women into factories while others found themselves working in banks and businesses, running civilian transport, delivering goods and services, joining the police force and later the fledging armed forces auxiliaries.

On the land the first priority was to maintain food supplies both for the fighting men and for the home population. Ships carrying grain and other imported food-stuffs on which Britain had come to rely in pre-war years were now the prime target for German U boats. Land that had been taken out of food production had quickly to be brought back into use, and women were for the first time officially called upon to do a man's job. And if still not seen by many men as equals, their role was unde-niably as important to the country as that of men. Dorothy Chalmers, working on a Cheshire Farm in 1915, sums up the attitude of many women:

Some people tell me that I shall not be able to go on with my farm work in the winter, because it will make my hands so bad. But I intend to stick to it. Our men don't stop fighting in the cold weather, and neither shall I.

The Board of Agriculture, along with County War Agricultural Committees and, later, Women's Agricultural Committees, formed various organisations with the purpose of producing materials both for the direct prosecution of the war and for sustaining the civilian population. The Women's Forage Corp, set up in 1915, helped to produce the enormous quantities of fodder required for the horses used in France – a staggering 5000 tons per day towards the war's end.

The principal agencies for the organisation of women workers on the land were the Women's National Land Service Corps, the Land Service Corp and the Women's Farm

Miss Rawle of Chittlehampton in Devon c.1916 wearing a long coat, thick black boots, black leggings and a broad brimmed hat – typical Land Army attire.

Women scything weeds at Lamerton in Devon during the First World War.

Their men gone to the war, these women at East-the-Water in Bideford, Devon, took over the work in the timber yard in 1916.

and Garden Union. In 1917 a single entity, the Women's Land Army was established with three units: agriculture, timber and forage, and by this date there were over a quarter of a million women working as farm labourers, with over 20 000 in the Women's Land Army itself.

In villages, on farms and in cottage gardens women, without being members of any organisation, simply got on with their lives, each contributing in their own way to sustaining the British way of life against a background of fear of the 'invading Hun', and worry for their menfolk fighting abroad, with the dread prospect of the telegram arriving bringing news of the death of a loved one. Though not all would mourn:

One women with a very bad husband owned frankly that she would not be sorry if he were killed. 'But I 'spose he'll be spared, and others as'd missed'll be taken, for that's the way of things. It's the only time as I and the children 'ad peace. The war's been a 'appy time for us.'

As the war progressed food shortages became acute although country people at least had ample access to the wild plants that had sustained their forebears in times of need. Children played their part too – school lessons were abandoned so they might bring in the harvest and playgrounds were given over to the growing of vegetables. Women too old for physical work gave their time to knitting gloves and balaclavas for the troops, or engaged in fund raising. In 1917 the pupils from Axminster school sent 2000 bunches of primroses to Exeter for sale on behalf of Red Cross funds and

Fourteen year old Marjorie Rees helps her blacksmith father at the forge while her two older brothers are away at the Front.

Wearing her Land Army uniform a young girl rides out from Teigngrace Farm in Devon in 1915.

sphagnum moss was collected and packed for dispatch to field hospitals for use as wound dressings. Eggs, potatoes and other vegetables were also sent to the Armed Forces and all children were encouraged to save their pocket money for War Funds.

Along with their traditional farming duties, the role of women in nursing came to the fore during the war, the greatest number of uniformed nurses being those trained by The Red Cross or St John Ambulance who also recruited and trained VAD nurses.

The most radical departure in the employment of women came in their direct use within the military itself. An early unit was the Women's Emergency Corps founded in 1914, followed by the Women's Legion in 1915. In 1917 the Women's Army Auxiliary Corps and the Women's Royal Naval Service were followed in 1918 by the Women's Royal Air Force. While performing duties from secretaries to cooks, these women also took on duties closer to the front line as ambulance drivers. Indeed it was their growing familiarity with early motor vehicles that reinforced the notion that women were just as capable as men, if not more so, in such roles. Other organisations, such as the Women's Volunteer Motor Drivers, founded in 1918, furthered this idea. As Pam Lomax points out in her paper on the subject: 'The W.V.M.D set out to give women drivers the finishing course in road experience that no garage could supply; it aimed to enhance members' driving skills to the standard where they would be acceptable to the Red Cross and other branches of national service.'

Women and girls collecting sphagnum moss on Dartmoor during the First World War. When dried it was used in the antiseptic treatment of wounds.

Women Red Cross drivers at work on their ambulances behind the lines on the Western Front in 1918. A photograph by Olive Edis one of the first women to be accorded official war artist status.

THE FARMER'S WIFE

The 1914–18 war was a cataclysm in which millions died and from which all that went before was subject to change. As the historian A.L. Rowse has it:

The War brought all that life of habit to a sudden full stop, held it suspended, breathless for a full four years in the shadow of its wing, and meanwhile set in being motions and tendencies which came to full flood the moment the War was over and swept away the old landmarks in a tide of change. The old social structure has at length been broken, like a pitcher at the well, the pieces dispersed. And the same with many of the old customs and ways.

A report in the *Daily Express* in February 1917 succinctly describes the effects of the war on the public perception of women:

The war has brought into being many different aspects of women as worker, organiser, and general helper, but the greatest innovation of all is the woman soldier, recognised by the military authorities, uniformed, living in camps beside the men, under the same conditions as to food and lodging, and working day in, day out, under strict discipline. There is not the smallest doubt that, had it been suggested that women should undertake work of this kind during the first months of the war, there would have been a great outcry, and the busybodies would have shaken their heads and said it was asking the impossible.

Within months of the war's end in 1918 the Representation of the People Act enfranchised women over the age of 30 and in 1928 women received the vote on the same terms as men.

This book has been devoted to the woman whose working traditions lay in the land and in her role as wife to the farmer, and to those who laboured on the land. It is she who for hundreds of years exemplified the life of almost all the working poor. The Mysterious Lady so seldom recorded by history, now emerges into the light.

The last word goes to Flora Annie Steel in 'Woman Makes a New World' published in the *Daily Express* in November 1918:

Verily and indeed, if we women have done something in this war, the war has done more for us women. It has taught us to recognise ourselves, to justify our existence. Ideas that for the most part were but the baseless fabric of a dreamer's vision have taken form and the world is fresh and new for womanhood. Why, our very carriage is different, as anyone with eyes can see! As Kipling puts it, we walk now as if we owned ourselves, and we stand closer to each other.

Bibliography

Ayres, Jack. *Paupers and Pig Killers. The Diary of William Holland 1799–1818*. Alan Sutton, Gloucester 1984.

Blythe, Ronald. *Akenfield*. Book Club Associates, London 1972.

Bourne, George. *Change in the Village*. Penguin, London 1984.

Bradley, Richard. *The Country Housewife and Lady's Director*. London 1732.

Brown, Martin. *Australia Bound! The Story of Westcountry Connections*. Ex Libris Press, Bradford on Avon 1988.

Butler, Simon. *Goodbye Old Friend. A sad Farewell to the Working Horse*. Halsgrove, Wellington 2010.

Butler, Simon. *The War Horses. The Tragic Fate of a Million Horses in the First World War*. Halsgrove, Wellington 2010.

Chase, A.W. *Dr Chase's Recipes, or Information for Everybody*. Ann Arbor, Michigan 1866.

Cobbett, William. *Cottage Economy*. Oxford Paperbacks, Oxford 1979.

Cobbett, William. *Rural Rides*. Pierrot Publishing Ltd, 1980.

Dickens, Charles. *The Complete Works of Charles Dickens*. Delphi Classics Kindle edition 2011.

Evans, George Ewart. *The Pattern Under the Plough*. Faber & Faber, London 1966.

Evans, George Ewart. *Ask the Fellows Who Cut the Hay*. Faber & Faber, London 1965.

Farmer, Virginia. *Roman Farm Management. The Treatises of Cato and Varro*. MacMillan & Co. London 1913.

Fitzherbert, Anthony. *Boke of Husbandrie*. London 1534.

Francatelli, Charles Elme, *The Cook's Guide and Housekeeper's and Butler's Assistant*. Richard Bentley, London 1863.

Glyde, John. *Suffolk in the Nineteenth Century*. Simpkin, Marshall & Co., Ipswich 1856.

Grayzel, Susan R. *Women and the First World War*. Pearson Education Ltd, Harlow 2002.

Hardy, Thomas. *The Romantic Adventures of a Milkmaid*. MacMillan & Co. London 1913.

Hardy, Thomas. *Tess of the d'Urbervilles*. Bounty Books, 2001.

Houlston & Sons (publisher). Enquire Within Upon Everything. London 1856.

Hughes, Anne. *The Diary of a Farmer's Wife 1796-1797*. The Good Life Press 2009.

Hunt, Irvine. *Lakeland Yesterday Volume 1*. Smith Settle Ltd, Otley 2002.

James, David and Todd, A.C. *Ever Westward the Land*. Exeter University Press 1986.

Jeffries, Richard. *Round About a Great Estate*. Ex Libris Press, Bradford on Avon 1987.

Jenner, Edward. *An Inquiry into the Causes and Effects of the Variolae Vaccinae*. Sampson Low, London 1798.

Kent & Co (publisher) *The Family Save All. A System of Secondary Cookery*. London 1861.

Lucy, Donna M. *Photographing Montana 1894–1928*. Mountain Press Publishing Company, Missoula 2010.

Lomax, Pam. 'Women Volunteer Motor Drivers' in the *Journal of the Cornwall Association of Local Historians*. Truro 2008.

Markham, Gervase. *The English Huswife*. London 1615.

Marlow, Joyce ed. *Women and the Great War*. Virago, London 1999.

Martin, E.W. *The Shearers and the Shorn*. Routledge and Kegan Paul, London 1965.

Marshall, William. *The Rural Economy of Gloucestershire*. Debrett, London 1796.

McLynn, Frank. *Wagons West. The Epic Story of America's Overland Trails*. Pimlico, London 2003.

Miller, Marion Mills. *Practical Suggestions for Mother and Housewife*. 1910.

Mitford, Mary Russell. *Our village: sketches of rural character and scenery*. George Whittaker, London 1828.

Moxon, Elizabeth. *English Housewifry Exemplified*. 1764.

Raffald, Elizabeth. The Experienced English Housekeeper. Baldwin, London 1769.

Sayer, Karen. 'Field-faring women' in *Women's History Review*. University of Luton 1993.

Smith, Guy. *A History of the NFU. From Campbell to Kendall*. Halsgrove, Wellington 2008.

Stanes, Robin. *The Husbandry of Devon and Cornwall*. Privately published, Exeter 2008.

Stephens, Henry. *The Book of the Farm*. Blackwood & Sons, London 1844.

Stopes, Charlotte Carmichael. *British Freewomen: Their Historical Privilege*. Swan Sonnenschein, London. 1894.

Storey, Neil R. and Housego, Molly. *Women in the First World War*. Shire Publications, Oxford 2011.

Street, Sean ed. *A Land Remembered. Recollections of Life in the Countryside 1880–1914*. Claremont Books, London 1996.

Thane, Pat. 'Happy Families: A Report Prepared for the British Academy'. The British Academy, London 2010.

Thompson, Flora. *Lark Rise to Candleford*. Penguin, London 1973.

Torr, Cecil. *Small Talk at Wreyland*. Cambridge University Press, Cambridge 1918.

Various authors. *The Halsgrove Community History Series*. see www.halsgrove.com

Verdon, Nicola. 'The employment of women and children in agriculture: a reassessment of agricultural gangs in nine-teenth-century Norfolk.' *The Agricultural History Review* Vol. 49, No. 1, 2001.

Walton, Jack. *The Last Farewell. Devon Convicts Transported to Australia 1782–1821*. Australian Scholarly Publishing 2003.

Wigby, Frederick C. *Just a Country Boy*. George Reeve Ltd, Wymondham 1976.

Woods, Stephen. *Dartmoor Farm*. Halsgrove, Tiverton 2003.

Woollacott, Angela. *On Her Their Lives Depend*. University of California Press, Berkeley 1994.

Woolley, Hannah *The Queen-like Closet or Rich Cabinet*. London 1672.